rootedness

rootedness

reflections for young architects

JUHANI PALLASMAA

Peter MacKeith, Editor

WILEY

Registered Office(s)
John Wiley & Sons, Inc., 111 River Street, Hoboken, NJ 07030, USA

John Wiley & Sons Ltd, The Atrium, Southern Gate, Chichester, West Sussex, PO19 8SQ, UK

For details of our global editorial offices, customer services, and more information about Wiley products visit us at www.wiley.com.

Wiley also publishes its books in a variety of electronic formats and by print-on-demand. Some content that appears in standard print versions of this book may not be available in other formats.

Library of Congress Cataloging-in-Publication Data Applied for:

Hardback ISBN: 9781394217052

Cover Design: Wiley

SKY10066210_013124

CONTENTS

WALKING IN THE FOREST
Editor's Foreword

The origins of this book are rooted in both the relative immediacy
of the last five years and in the superlative lifelong experience of its
author – Juhani Pallasmaa.

I first asked Juhani to consider joining the faculty at the Fay Jones
School of Architecture and Design, University of Arkansas as a
visiting professor in 2017; we were able to formalize the necessary
arrangements for the spring of 2018, when he arrived in Fayetteville
as the Fay Jones School's distinguished visiting professor in architecture and design for the semester.

As Juhani describes in the Introduction, in asking him to teach
within the school's interdisciplinary first-year curriculum, I had
suggested that he might consider the stance, if not the template,
of Rainer Maria Rilke's small book, *Letters to a Young Poet*, through
a series of lectures – presented almost as confiding letters – to the
beginning students, addressing the newly arrived students' outlooks
and perspectives on architecture and design. Juhani undertook
this role and responsibility with typical commitment and vigor,
and I remember well how he sat at a small table in the front of the
school's lecture hall each week during the term, reading the texts
now published here. I also remember that the lectures soon became
crowded with students from the upper years and faculty from all pro-
grams – suddenly everyone understood themselves as a beginning
student and needed a seat!

From the start, we had discussed the conversion of these lectures
into a small book itself, and this is now that publication, emerging out of a simultaneously slowed and intense period of time and
history – pandemic, recession, political crisis, and war. To remember
the spring of 2018 can seem dreamlike in retrospect.

But the vibrancy of those lectures now resonates in the printed
pages. For the origins, motivations and expressions of this book are

equally rooted in the long lived experience of its author, and these roots are deeper, more substantial, and durable – certainly capable of bridging across the interval between their initial spoken presentation and their printed quality now. Indeed, this "rootedness" – the necessary centering of identity and awareness, of sensitivity and intellect, to act creatively and responsibly in architecture and the arts – is precisely the central proposition of the author, as relevant to the curious reader now as it was to beginning student in 2018. In this sense, the book is both autobiographical and educational, both confession and primer, and the dual qualities intertwine and mutually reinforce one another for a superlative richness and density.

To continue further would be to presume upon the author, but I will suggest one last extended framework for reading these reflections. As cosmopolitan and well-traveled as Juhani Pallasmaa is, he is utterly rooted in his Finnish homeland, physically, emotionally, and metaphorically. As he described to me in a published interview in 2005, "My travels have strengthened my appreciation of individuals and achievements of other cultures, on all continents, but also reinforced my deep mental connection with the Nordic landscape. I can say sincerely that the more I have traveled, the more attached I feel to the Finnish natural and cultural soil. Often, in these fantastic destinations, before I fall asleep, I have an image of a view out onto a lake or deep into the Finnish forest."[1]

1
Juhani Pallasmaa, Encounters: Essays in Architecture, Peter MacKeith, ed. (Helsinki: Rakennustieto, 2005), 21.

To be clear, what the reader will not encounter here in *Rootedness* is a guide to the Finnish forest or an advocacy of "an architecture of the forest." Rather, I suggest that what the reader may encounter in reading is the conceptual, or mental, experience of walking in the forest, of a slowed sense of time, of invigorated breathing, of a deliberate movement (intellectually and emotionally) across, and through a diverse and dense terrain, oriented by significant recurring trees and boulders, and the cosmological elements of the sun, moon, or stars overhead – or, in the case of this book, oriented by significant, recurring intellectual companions and literary references, and the cosmological elements of time, history, human nature (including our mortality), and our presence in the universe.

This is a deep Finnish dreamworld, mythical perhaps, but one from which Juhani's sensibilities and writings emerge, one simultaneously geographical, cultural, intellectual, and emotional, and one meriting a further degree of larger exploration. The vision of Finland as an "Ultima Thule" – an end of the world – populates the historical and cultural imagination. Indeed, the perception and valuation of the

Finnish wilderness as a virtuous periphery, and as a source for artistic and cultural renewal, even as a source of national identity, extends well back into European history.

Undeniably, the Finnish forest wilderness was the source for artistic and cultural renewal for the developing cultural (and ultimately national) identity of the Finnish people, as these emerged throughout the nineteenth century and led to a proud declaration of the independent nation-state in 1917. But the forest wilderness has been the same deep resource of identity for so many Finnish artists, architects, composers, and writers from the nineteenth century until the present day.

In this way, Pallasmaa's beckoning to walk with him in the forest of identity – a sylvan experience both personal and cultural – has its antecedents and companions. For instance, as recorded in the journals of Juhani Aho, the nineteenth-century Finnish author and journalist, Finnish artists of that time found a forest of stilled light and suspended time. In the summer of 1892, Aho undertook an excursion to the eastern Finnish region of Karelia, together with his wife Venny Soldan and the painter Eero Järnefelt. In search of the sources of the emerging Finnish identity in the forested landscapes of the region – the original landscapes of the Finnish myth-epic poem *The Kalevala* – Aho recorded his impressions in travel books and also in written vignettes, short intense evocations of place and mood he entitled *Lastuja* ("shavings").

One of Aho's vignettes, "Synkän korven sydämeen (Into the Heart of a Gloomy Deep Forest)," is a poetic confession from the excursion subtitled "Luonnonkuvauksia Raja-Karjalasta (Nature Descriptions from Borderland Karelia)." In the depths of the Karelian forest, Aho describes a shift in the travelers' experience of time, a palpable slowing of its passage: *"Time seems to lose its measure, the journey along this pine barren seems to have been indefinitely long, even though it has not yet last a full hour. And I wonder how long we may have been sitting here resting, although not yet five minutes have elapsed since we placed ourselves here."*[2]

If this expansion of duration in the forest, this slowing of boreal time, into a "measureless" sensation is an absolute condition of our experience of nature, as Aho suggests in 1892, here I suggest to the contemporary reader of the following pages of *Rootedness: Reflections for Young Architects* that this is the absolute condition of the experience of this book.

2

Heikki Kirkinen and Hannes Sihvo, *The Kalevala: An Epic of Finland and All Mankind* (Helsinki: The Finnish-American Cultural Center/The League of Finnish-American Societies, 1985), 44.

Allow yourself, then, to enter this forest of thought, reflection, and expression that is this book, to walk alongside the author for a chapter, to encounter over the course of reading one chapter, and then another, and then another, recurring figures inhabiting that landscape – Joseph Brodsky, for instance, Alvar Aalto, of course, Groucho Marx, surprisingly, and unsurprisingly, Rilke himself. As well, the author walks in spiraling paths, tracing and retracing his steps, his patterns of thought, and his propositions in deliberate recurrence.

There is a density to this forest of thought, to be sure; in Finnish, this quality is understood as "*tiiveys*," a condensation as much of emotion as it is of material. And there is an animated quality of lived experience expressed in every sentence and word in that spirit; in Finnish, this qualitative understanding is understood as "*elämys*." *Elämys*: the Finnish word translates into English as "experience," but immediately loses its depth and potency in the translation. The Finnish word connotes an enriched understanding of experience – of a space or place, of a moment in time – one that is not merely enjoyable in a directly physical way, or esthetic in a cognitive awareness of forms and colors, but occurs to a profound depth of suspended time and emotional resonance. For an architect, such an experience often compels an immediate desire to know how such a place was constructed, then designed, and then conceived; to seek out how such a phenomenon was reified, and perhaps, in time, to be afforded the opportunity to evoke a similar depth of experience in others through their own designed construction. It is this experience I wish also for the reader of *Rootedness*, one both of the forest and in the forest.

As a tangible coda to these propositions, the architect's most recent constructed work may be illustrative. In summer, 2023, in central Finland, in forested peatlands of Pehkusuo, near the Kuivajärvi Lake, at the Hyytiälä Forestry Field Station of the University of Helsinki, where scientific research related to forest management and climate change is advanced, Pallasmaa centered an artistic work in the landscape of his design entitled "*After the Rain*." Part of "Periferia/Periphery," a commissioned group exhibition at the field station, "*After the Rain*" is a 36 m diameter circle configured along its circumference every 30° by 12 thin vertical steel rods glowing in the colors of the spectrum. "A rainbow drawn into a circle," as Pallasmaa describes it, in effect a drawing directly into nature, gently but distinctly marking the earth and the surrounding forest, registering the presence of light, wind, and the nearby lake waters, and intensifying the understanding of the specific place and its geographical history. "Twelve is the dividing line of the clock, calendar and compass," Pallasmaa relates, "and through this, the work becomes a dimension of place and time. The blue color comes to the north, so the work can be used as a giant compass."[3]

Walk with Juhani Pallasmaa; with this sense of time, with this sense of orientation, enter the forest that is *Rootedness: Reflections for Young Architects*.

Editor's Acknowledgements

Gratitude and appreciation must be given to Katri Sola, who assisted in the production of the manuscript and in the preparation of the images for this book, and to the editorial and production team at Wiley for their commitment, stamina, sensitivity, and patience.

Gratitude, appreciation, and affection must be given to Juhani Pallasmaa for the privilege of the editorial role, for the opportunity to collaborate once again, and for the abiding friendship of more than 30 years.

3
"Maan Korvessa (In the heart of the land)," Pia Parkkinen, Culture Section, Helsingin Sanomat, June 30, 2023 (translation the author).

HAILUOTO U 780

PROLOGUE

In the Wake of Rilke's *Letters to a Young Poet*

In the spring of 2018, as I was beginning to think about the contents of my agreed teaching assignment at the Fay Jones School of Architecture and Design in Fayetteville, Arkansas, the dean of the school, Professor Peter MacKeith, brought to me in Helsinki the little book entitled *Letters to a Young Poet*.[1] These famous letters were written by Rainer Maria Rilke, one of the greatest poets of the modern era, who was born in 1875 and died of leukemia at the young age of 51 in 1926.

"Why don't you approach your lectures to our students through something like this?" my friend suggested to me. As I knew the book very well, I first felt a slight shiver through my body. I have often spoken about the book to students across the world as well as about many other writings by its author (in fact, I already had three copies of the book in my library: German, English, and Finnish). In other lectures and throughout my writings, I have spoken often of Rilke's poetry and of his extensive poetic correspondence with numerous people. Rilke's superb book on the French sculptor-genius *Auguste Rodin*[2] (Rilke actually worked as the secretary of the artist, whom he had greatly admired, in 1905–1906) and his stunning, quasi-autobiographical novel *The Notebooks of Malte Laurids Brigge*[3] have been essential references for me.

For me, Rilke has been one of the most amazing creative artists in modern history and culture, and the thought of trying to do anything echoing his writings felt like blasphemy. Yet, after a few minutes my second reaction was: "Juhani, you will be 82 later this year, and if you do not now dare to do anything that is suggested to you, you will never be able to do it." After all, Rilke was only 27 (55 years younger than I was at the time of my doubt) when he wrote the first one of his letters to Franz Xaver Kappus, the aspiring young poet. I also remembered a line from Rilke's eighth letter in their correspondence: "[. . .] Only someone who is ready for everything, who excludes nothing, not even the most enigmatical, will live the

1

Rainer Maria Rilke, *Letters to a Young Poet,* transl. by M.D. Herter Norton (New York and London: W. W. Norton & Company, 1934), reissued 1993.

2

Rainer Maria Rilke, *Rodin* (New York: Archipelago Books, 2004).

3

Rainer Maria Rilke, *The Notebooks of Malte Laurids Brigge* (New York and London: W. W. Norton & Company, 1992).

4

Rainer Maria Rilke, *Letters to a Young Poet*, op.cit., 68.

5

See, Juhani Pallasmaa, *One Week Workshop, Burial Urn for an Artist, Workshop Report*, Aleš Vodopivec and Klara Bonine, eds. (Ljubljana: University of Ljubljana, 2015).

6

Rainer Maria Rilke, *Duino Elegies*, transl. by David Young (New York: W. W. Norton & Company, 1978).

7

Rax Rinnekangas, *Muodonmuutos: yksinpuhelu Rainer Maria Rilkelle* [Metamorphosis: soliloquy with Rainer Maria Rilke] (Helsinki: Lurra Editions, 2006). Rilke lived in the La Reina Victoria Hotel in Ronda for three months in the winter 1912–13. Rinnekangas has also made a film *Luciferin viimeinen elämä* [The last life of Lucifer], 2013, which has numerous references to and quotes from Rilke.

8

Paul Valéry, *Dialogues*, trans. William McCausland Stewart (New York: Pantheon Books, 1956), XIII.

relation to another as something alive and will himself draw exhaustively from his own existence."[4]

In fact, this would not be the first time that I encountered and engaged with Rilke in a teaching situation. In 2016, I led a week-long workshop at the University of Ljubljana in Slovenia,[5] in which I gave my students the assignment to design the burial ceremony and urn of Rilke on the Duino Coast on the northern Adriatic Sea near Slovenia. The poet had stayed in the Duino Castle in 1910 for some time as the guest of Princess Marie von Thurn und Taxis, and there he began to write his poetic ten-part masterpiece *The Duino Elegies*,[6] which was ultimately published in 1923. For the studio exercise, two other artists were given as optional "clients" to the students: Giorgio Morandi, the great painter of metaphysical still-lifes, and Alberto Giacometti, the existentialist Swiss–French sculptor.

As I thought more on the possibility, it occurred to me just how much of a constant companion Rilke has been for me. On that realization, I remembered that several years ago my friend Rax Rinnekangas – the Finnish writer, photographer, and filmmaker – had published a small book entitled *Metamorphoses: a soliloquy to Rainer Maria Rilke*.[7] As my friend describes the initial inspiration, he had stayed a night in a humble hotel in the historic Spanish town of Ronda, and, as he woke up in the morning, he noticed a small framed black-and-white portrait photograph on the wall opposite his bed and recognized it as the poet Rilke. He went down to the reception to ask why they had a photograph of the famous poet in the hotel room. The hotel concierge informed my friend that the poet had stayed in that room during 1912–1913, and my friend felt so intrigued by the coincidence of sleeping in the same bed as one of his literary idols that he decided to write a series of letters to Rilke, 82 years after the poet's premature death.

This is a touching example of how a great artist may live among us indefinitely, without boundaries. In this way, it makes perfect sense to start a correspondence with a person who is not physically among us, but who is most vividly present through his works. "An artist is worth a thousand centuries," writes Paul Valéry, another master poet whom Rilke admired.[8] Great artistic works – poems and novels as well as material works such as paintings, sculptures, and buildings – maintain their eternal sense of newness and freshness, and, through them, we can develop emotionally vivid relationships with our favorite artists, even though they might have lived hundreds of years ago. Reading a great novel with intense focus or gazing with equal intensity at a masterpiece of painting brings the author or artist back to life, standing next to the reader and viewer. Studying Vermeer's painting, *View of Delft* (1660–1661), alone in the gallery in the Mauritshuis in Delft, as close as the security will allow, I finally felt that I stood next to the Dutch painter, painting "the yellow spot," the yellow wall that Proust described so vividly in the novel *The Captive*.

I describe these events related with Rilke as examples of how we might become unexpectedly close to the great men and women artists of the past. With my eight reflections in this book, I wish to promote and stimulate such imaginative relations and encounters. One of the reasons why our sense of time and the layering of culture are flattening and diminishing in our era is that in the modern world "Life is only for the living," as T.S. Eliot regrets in his poetic masterpiece *Four Quartets*,[9] when, in fact, we should recognize the rich presence of the past in our everyday lives.

9
T. S. Eliot, *Four Quartets* (London: Faber & Faber Limited, 1944, 2001).

I do not intend to follow the themes of Rilke's *Letters to a Young Poet* in these reflections, but I will attempt to talk about architecture with the same sincerity and openness with which Rilke wrote about poetry in his letters to the young man. I will also try to evoke a densely layered consciousness in the histories of the arts, literature, and philosophical thought, and suggest what a young student of architecture and design might learn from areas of culture beyond the boundaries of the professional disciplines of architecture and design. Historical facts, knowledge, or thinking are not isolated atoms in a formless cloud of information, as digitalized bits; on the contrary, they form a dense network of causalities and interactions. This endless interaction and intertwining is crucial in all creative thoughts, and it makes knowledge even seemingly far from one's discipline useful in one's own work.

I wish to create a kind of a forest of thought in which the reader can become happily lost. The side note references are not given to show the extensiveness of my library; my numerous quotes are only intended to leave traces that the readers may follow beyond the contents of these condensed texts. To maintain the initial atmosphere of the lecture hall, I have used only the names of the persons whom I am discussing and/or quoting in the text, with only minimal notation of their profession or time period. Everything in these reflections arises from my 86 years of life experience, more than 60 of those as an architect, from my library of 10,000 books, and from my 106 circumnavigations of the globe (the figure is calculated from my total amount of flying hours; by today's passenger airplanes, one circumnavigation of the globe equals 48 hours of flight time).

And thus, to my dialogue with Rilke: in February 1903, the 27-year-old poet, already accomplished and lauded, received a letter from a young German man, Franz Xaver Kappus, who introduced himself as an aspiring poet, and then asked for advice on how to become a poet. (As it happened, Kappus had attended the same military officers school as Rilke, only several years later.) The letter had been in transit to Rilke for several weeks due to his rather mobile life within Europe. However, on February 17th, 1903, Rilke answered the letter of the unknown young man, and this became the first of ten letters that Rilke was to write to Kappus in response to the younger poet's letters during the following five years. Rilke's tenth and last letter was dated in Paris on the day after Christmas in 1908.

This famous correspondence forms the background and resonance for my talks, and I advise my readers to read *Letters to a Young Poet* and also Rilke's correspondence with his wife. The sculptor Clara Westhof (a number of these letters are on the painter Paul Cézanne[10]) as well as his letters to others, such as Auguste Rodin and many of his friends, admirers, supporters, and lovers of high esteem.[11] Rilke's correspondence in 1926, the last year of his life, with two notable Russian writers – Boris Pasternak and Marina Tsvetaeva – is also touching because of their mutual admiration.[12]

Altogether, letters are a special category of literature altogether, and Rilke's small book has many worthy companions, I can recommend the voluminous letters of Anton Chekhov – the Russian writer and playwright (especially the annotated volume format that puts the letters in their historical and social contexts[13]), the letters of Vincent van Gogh to his brother Theo,[14] as well as the letters of Paul Cézanne.[15] I even wish to highlight the curious correspondence between the poet T.S. Eliot and Groucho Marx – the eldest of the legendary Marx Brothers of early cinematic comedy, in *Groucho Marx Letters*,[16] to exemplify how totally different personalities can become friends. A remarkable recent correspondence is the exchange of letters between the authors J.M. Coetzee, the South African Nobel Laureate, and Paul Auster, the Brooklyn-centered American.[17]

Due to the intimacy of the literary medium, you can easily place yourself in the role of the recipient and read the letters as if they

10

Rainer Maria Rilke, *Letters on Cézanne*, Clara Rilke, ed. (New York: North Point Press, 1985).

11

Letters of Rainer Maria Rilke (W. W. Norton & Company, 1969).

12

Letters Summer 1926: Boris Pasternak, *Marina Tsvetaeva, Rainer Maria Rilke* (New York: New Review of Books, 2001).

13

Anton Chekhov, *Letters of Anton Chekhov*, Simon Karlinsky, ed. (New York: Harper & Row, 1973), 338.

14

Vincent van Gogh, *A Life in Letters* (London: Thames & Hudson, 2020).

15

Paul Cézanne, *The Letters of Paul Cézanne*, Alex Danchev, ed. (London: Thames & Hudson, 2013).

16

Groucho Marx, *The Groucho Letters: Letters From and To Groucho Marx* (New York: Simon & Schuster, 2007).

17

J. M. Coetzee and Paul Auster, *Here and Now: Letters 1913–18* (Helsinki: Tammi, 2013).

were addressed to you. In this way, you will never forget the lesson on literary restraint by Anton Chekhov in his letter to Maxim Gorki – a beginning writer at the time: "Your only fault is your lack of restraint and lack of grace. When someone expends the least amount of motion on a given action, that's grace. You tend to expend too much [. . .] Color and expressivity in nature descriptions are achieved through simplicity alone, through simple phrases like 'the sun sets', 'it grows dark', 'it began to rain'."[18] One can almost mentally touch the hand of the writer of a personal letter, and begin to ask him or her questions. You might even end up writing letters to your secret mentor – who may no longer be among the living – as my friend Rax was compelled to write to Rilke.

A last note on the recent unexpected reappearances of Rilke for me: after having given the first three of my lectures at the Fay Jones School, I visited a bookshop in Fayetteville with Peter MacKeith, and spotted a book by the biologist Edward O. Wilson, entitled *Letters to a Young Scientist*,[19] wherein Wilson advises the reader on biophilia, "the science and ethics of life."[20]

These unexpected encounters exemplify the phenomenon that a deep immersion in a subject will produce echoes, references, and parallels to that subject. This is not magic, although it may seem so: through the immersive process, your attention and eyesight simply become sharper and more focused in the area in which you are engaged, and you begin to recognize and receive connections and resonances that would have otherwise never occurred. While I was working on the manuscript for these lectures and this book, for instance, I received as a gift a book entitled *Letter to a Young Architect*,[21] by the Greek architect Alexandros N. Tombazis. While Tombazis does not mention Rilke and his letters, to my mind the gift was an almost logical result of my immersion in the literature of letters.

Letter-writing has an important place in my own development as an architect and educator. I have been an eager correspondent for decades, and, in the spring of 2018, I donated my correspondence files of roughly 1000 letters (27 meters of archival shelf space) to the Finnish National Archive. Due to the usual symmetry of correspondence, roughly half of these letters are of my hand. Until the onset of the digital era, I carefully filed my letters alphabetically and chronologically in large binders. A digital print of a careless and hurried contemporary letter, often containing mistakes in spelling and grammar, does not inspire anyone to file them, when compared with

18
Anton Chekhov, Letter to Aleksej Peskhkov (Maxim Gorki), January 3, 1899, in *Letters of Anton Chekhov*, op.cit.

19
Edward O. Wilson, *Letters to a Young Scientist* (New York and London: Liveright Publishing Corporation, 2013).

20
Edward O. Wilson, *Biophilia* (Cambridge, Massachusetts and London, England: Harvard University Press, 1984).

21
Alexandros N. Tombazis, *Letter to a Young Architect* (Athens: Libro Ltd, 2007).

carefully worded, typed, and composed letters, not to speak of letters written in beautiful longhand. Such is the hurried and fragmented nature of culture today, increasingly prosaic, or even meaningless, compounded by ever-increasing amounts of stimuli and entertainment. The architect-philosopher Paul Virilio observes that "the most important product of today's culture is speed"[22]; in agreement, I advise my students to resist the insidious erosion of meaning and value that results from haste and carelessness. Secrets and treasures can only be encountered slowly, attentively, and laboriously, and this is part of the value of letters and thinking toward our work through letters.

The overall title of my lectures, "Rootedness," echoes intentionally the beautiful title of the 1949 book *L'Enracinement*[23] (usually translated in English as "The Need for Roots") by the French social philosopher, writer, and mystic Simone Weil, who was an activist in the French Resistance during the World War II. The need for rootedness in the world, in culture, and in life, is evident in the contemporary condition of frenetic activity, alienation, and lack of focus.

Working on my nine lectures, I realized that reading *Letters to a Young Poet* becomes genuinely meaningful only when one knows enough of its writer. In the same way, I thought to begin my series of lectures by introducing myself and my work as an architect to my audience. In all cases, the background of the writer provides a distinct echo to the literary message, although many writers advise their readers to believe in the text, not the writer. As the Czech writer Milan Kundera argues, books are always wiser than their writers because they arise from "the wisdom of the novel."[24] In my view, there is a similar "wisdom of architecture" that we should identify and heed. All great pieces of architecture are surely "wiser" than their designers, as true creative work always reaches something beyond the conscious grasp and understanding of its maker. Essentially, studying architecture is learning this secret wisdom of the art form and feeling at ease with that important wisdom.

As I have grown to live my life as an architect, I have grown to experience the world through an architect's eyes, sensibilities, and mindset. In the first of my lectures in Fayetteville, I presented my design work as an architect-designer in a survey entitled "Thought and Form: Twelve Themes in my Work." These themes are not a program or a preconception: I have simply noticed that I have returned repeatedly to certain themes, which are part of my persona and

22

Paul Virilio, *Katoamisen Estetiikka* [the aesthetics of disappearance] (Tampere: Gaudeamus, 1994).

23

Simone Weil, *L'Enracinement* (Gallimard, 1949).

24

Milan Kundera, *Romaanin Taide* [The Art of the Novel] (Helsinki: WSOY, 1986), 165.

history, or the way I am related with my world. In 2011, I closed the design activities of my office in Helsinki after having finalized my last architectural project in Lapland – the Rovaniemi Art Museum and Concert Hall called *Korundi*. After that date, I have only written, lectured, taught, and participated in competition juries in different countries. While I may have changed my designer profession to writing, in truth, this is now simply the best means for me to continue my curiosity for and interest in the mysteries of the world and art.

In this book format of my original 2018 lectures, the basic structure and contents of the lectures have been maintained, but the manuscripts and subsequent editing process has allowed for clarifications, refinements, and slight expansions. As the original introductory survey lecture of my architectural work consisted of more than one hundred and fifty paired images – too many to be included in this book – and as my writings also arise from my experiences as a designer, I decided to replace that visual introduction to my design work with a personal confession on my work as a writer at the end of these chapters as a final piece. That final reflection is provided here as an epilogue entitled "A Confession." This personal approach reflects the fact that I have not studied philosophy academically, but have come to my understandings and observations of this most important way of "being in the world" through experience, reading, close observation, and shared dialogues over the course of life. *Rootedness* is a correspondence, then, with students and with Rilke, but also with my past, present, and future.

EL TAJIN
23-12-75

Selfhood, Friendships, and the World

Consider this quote from one of my favorite architectural writers – the great Argentinian poet Jorge Luis Borges: "A man sets himself the task of portraying the world. Over the years he fills a given surface with images of provinces and kingdoms, mountains, bays, ships, islands, fish, rooms, instruments, heavenly bodies, and people. Shortly before he dies, he discovers that this patient labyrinth of lines is a drawing of his own face."[1]

My favorite architecture books are not books on architecture or by architects; the most important architecture books in my library are novels, poems, and books on and by writers, artists, philosophers, and film directors, as well as books on the sciences – from biology and psychology to neuroscience and physics. These books are not about architecture as a separate discipline, but about houses, man-made spaces, places, and situations as frames of authentic life. In particular, biographies of film directors bring us especially close to describing the work of architects, as cinema is entangled with life, human situations, and actions in much the same way as architecture. Architecture books usually present buildings as estheticized objects, whereas literature, film, and paintings portray them as backgrounds and frames of lived and experienced life.

During my student years, I classified my books as architecture books and "other" books. After a few years of rather intense reading, I realized that my category of "other books" revealed essences of architecture better than the books written especially for the field. Soon, I understood that all books are books about architecture, as architecture is an inseparable part of the human condition and fate; we live in and through architecture, and architecture provides the most significant frames and horizons of experiencing and understanding the world and the human condition.

1

Jorge Luis Borges, *The Secret Books* (Stony Creek: Leetes Island Books, 1999), 7.

Rootedness: Reflections for Young Architects. First edition. Juhani Pallasmaa. Edited by Peter MacKeith.
© 2024 John Wiley & Sons Ltd. Published 2024 by John Wiley & Sons Ltd.

2

Rainer Maria Rilke, *The Notebooks of Malte Laurids Brigge* (New York and London: W. W. Norton & Co., 1993), 26.

Rilke makes a significant statement on the task of writing poetry, and his observation surely applies to architecture, as well as to all authentic works of art: "Verses are not simply feelings, they are experiences."[2] Resounding this insight, the American philosopher John Dewey convincingly points out in his seminal book *Art as Experience* that a work of art emerges and exists through, and in, its individual experience. This surely also applies to architecture; and, in fact, one of Dewey's examples is the experience of the Parthenon: "By common consent, the Parthenon is a great work of art. Yet, it has esthetic standing only as the work becomes an experience for a human being [. . .] Art is always the product in experience for a human being [. . .] Art is always the product in experience of an interaction of human beings with their environment. Architecture is a notable instance of the reciprocity of the results in this interaction [. . .] The reshaping of subsequent experience by architectural works is more direct and more extensive than in the case of any art [. . .] They not only influence the future, but they record and convey the past."[3]

3

John Dewey, *Art as Experience* (New York: Putnam's: Minton, Balch & Company, 1934), 4–231.

In the world, we and our actions are always *placed*, and this *placeness* usually implies architecture in some form. The arts, in general, offer both dramatic and intimate views to the human condition; the art of architecture situates that human condition in the world.

As a student, I began to admire the touching artistic presentations of human figures in paintings, depicted as individuals or as groups of figures in a legendary or mythological context, or in an historical event, and then as an individual or as a group of figures in a room, a building, or an urban setting. For decades now, I have studied paintings by Giotto, Duccio di Buoninsegna, and other painters of the Siena School of the early Italian Renaissance. Time and again, in particular, the paintings of Fra Angelico have provided inspirational insight into the relationship between human beings and architecture. The Florentine artist's depictions of the simultaneous presentations of exteriors and interiors are especially meaningful demonstrations of the continuum of the inner and outer worlds, the continuity of space, the complementarity of the inside and the outside, and the duality of the material and the mental.

Whenever I have wanted to gain inspiration for any design task, I hardly ever sought examples of contemporary architecture in comparable situations; almost always I have sought my inspiration in these early Renaissance painterly representations. In these paintings, buildings are depicted almost as human figures, as if they also had a capacity to breathe and speak. The equality and dialog between the human figure and the architectural place are equally inspiring in historical iconic paintings, which I also often have studied to focus my perception and mindset for design work. The very same approach applies to cinema, as I have said previously, as an equally powerful art of the human condition and, in my view, the closest art form to architecture, related through the concept of existential, lived space. In my book entitled *The Architecture of Image: Existential Space in Cinema*, I explore the central role of existential, lived space in both architecture and cinema and the parallels and interactions of cinematic and architectural space; these are seminal concepts for me, further elaborated in these reflections.[4] The relationship across time between the paintings of the early Renaissance and the highest achievements of modern cinema may seem distant or tenuous, but I perceive an important correspondence for anyone working in architecture.

Architecture is often understood and taught as a utilitarian and formal discipline outside of us – as something that is "out there" in a material, objective, and autonomous world. Additionally, in our quasi-rational era, the practice of architecture is increasingly seeking an objectified and externalized scientific grounding. Yet, I want to propose that the real, and perhaps the only, source of a poetic architectural sensibility and creative capacity is one's selfhood – our own individual minds, our personal histories, and experiences – each of us as unique human stories and fates. To mold and cast our lives from the shapeless clay of our given individual conditions in the world is a human necessity, but to do so as architects and artists is a special circumstance and obligation.

In *The Notebooks of Malte Laurids Brigge*, Rilke advises us: "In writing poetry, one is always aided and even carried away by the rhythm of exterior things; for the lyrical cadence is that of nature: of the waters, the wind, the night. But to write rhythmic prose one must go deep into oneself, and find the anonymous and multiple rhythm of the blood. Prose needs to be built like a cathedral; there one is truly without a name, without ambition, without help: on scaffoldings, alone with one's consciousness."[5] This is also the fate of the architect; as a maker of buildings, you are also alone "on scaffoldings, alone with your consciousness." You must maintain your solitude in the middle of the complexities of life, surrounded by life and other people, and, I would add, as our work always takes place in a historical continuum, amid the accumulated life of all time. We need to be humble and courageous, at the same time, to acknowledge our work and to set ourselves to work in that cultural and temporal continuum.

4
Juhani Pallasmaa, *The Architecture of Image: Existential Space in Cinema* (Helsinki: Rakennustieto Oy), 2002.

5
Rainer Maria Rilke, *The Notebooks of Malte Laurids Brigge* (New York and London, W. W. Norton & Co., 1993).

6

Ludwig Wittgenstein, *Culture and Value*, Revised edition, G.H. von Wright, ed. (Oxford, UK: Blackwell Publishing, 2002), 24e.

7

Mark Johnson, *The Meaning of the Body: Aesthetics of Human Understanding* (Chicago and London: The University of Chicago Press, 2007).

8

Maurice Merleau-Ponty, *The Primacy of Perception*, James H. Edie, ed. (Evanston, Illinois: Northwestern University Press, 2000), 162.

Ludwig Wittgenstein – one of the most significant philosophers of the last century – confesses: "Work in philosophy – like work in architecture in many respects – is really more work on oneself. On one's own conception. On how one sees things."[6] The philosopher's lesson is clear in extension for our work in architecture and design: architecture is fundamentally thinking, not necessarily conceptual and verbal thinking, but embodied, sensory, and existential thinking, thinking through one's sense of being. Architecture is existential thinking and sensing human existence in the world – existence in space and time in general, but truly particular in place and situation. Architecture is also simultaneously a process of personal identification – a fusion of one's own experiences and growing self-awareness with the constructed settings and situations in which that growth occurs. Architecture is being an individual in constant encounter with the world – the delicate sensing and felt awareness of being in the world.

We normally assume that thinking is a purely cerebral activity of the brain, but this is a limited understanding, as several contemporary philosophers contend. Mark Johnson, among them, asserts that, "All thinking is embodied activity."[7] Maurice Merleau-Ponty, my favorite philosopher, argues this general proposition on behalf of artistic work writing,[8] "A painter takes his body with him. It is inconceivable that a bodiless mind could paint." But it is even more impossible that a bodiless mind could conceive architecture, or even think about it, as architecture is directly engaged with our embodied existence. Architecture is a continuation and extension of our bodies and minds, memories, and imaginations. We live in the "flesh of the world," to use Merleau-Ponty's even more provocative expression. How could we think of architecture without our existential body that generates it and gives it all its dimensions and meanings? At its most abstract and poetic moment, architecture reifies our existence and domicile in the world, mediating between our existence and the world and between our earthly and cosmic realities. Architecture fuses us with the world in its substance – a substantiation shared by us and our structures and constructions.

In my view, this realization of the embodiment of thought and our substantial presence in the world is the essence of the process of education: we learn to be both in the world and of the world. Information, both learned and acquired, and experiences and skills gradually condense around the students' understanding of themselves, of their selfhood. The development of this selfhood is at the very core of learning, and only lessons that have become part of oneself are useful in creative work. When gathering knowledge and experiences, we are simultaneously constructing both our world and our sense of self – our selfhood, that is, the significance of the mirror image in the Borges text with which I began this reflection. Our unconscious self-identity and understanding of selfhood, in relation to the natural, historical, cultural, social, and poetic worlds, is the sieve through which our experiences are filtered and evaluated.

Creative capacity does not arise from an external source as an imposed quality, as that would be only bound to echo what already exists, nor do the poetic and existential qualities of architecture arise from pure information or categorical knowledge. Information and knowledge are about what exists, but art and architecture are about what could be. We need knowledge for the technicalities, practicalities, and legalities of our work, but for the creative dimension, we need condensed and mature internalized understanding – what can only be called wisdom. This open possibility and invitation is essential in all creative works. To see and sense the nonexistent, we need wisdom. As Rilke maintains in one of his letters, "Art is not a little selective sample of the world, it is a transformation of the world, an endless transformation towards the good."[9] Wisdom is always the ultimate goal of teaching, but always the most difficult goal to achieve because it requires a deep collaboration between the teacher and the student.

To say this more declaratively: information and knowledge are of little value in true creative work; only experiences and skills that have become integrated with one's sense of being, one's self-identity, are of real use in this search for artistic meaning and expression. Also, irrespective of your experiences and abilities, any new creative task always returns you back to the beginning to a new search for the means of expression. This is true even for those with great experience and knowledge. Once in the early 1980s, I dined with the great Basque sculptor Eduardo Chillida – one of the most architectural of sculptors, and during the meal, he said: "I have never had any use of what I have done before when I begin to work on a new piece of sculpture." [10] This is an expression of amazing humility and open-mindedness, from an exceptional sculptor in his own right, and also one who once collaborated on a book with the philosopher Martin Heidegger – a central figure in twentieth century thought.[11]

In one of his letters to his sculptor wife Clara Westhoff, Rilke memorably describes the solitary and even dangerous path of the artist: "After all, works of art are always the result of one's having been in

9
Rainer Maria Rilke, Letter to Jacob Baron Uexkull, Paris, August 19, 1909. *Rainer Maria Rilke, Hiljainen taiteen sisin: kirjeitä vuosilta 1900–1926* (The silent innermost core of art: letters 1900–1926), Liisa Enwald, ed. (Helsinki: TAI-teos, 1997), 41.

10
Private conversation at a dinner in Helsinki in 1987 between Chillida and the writer.

11
Martin Heidegger, *Die Kunst und der Raum* (Erker-Verlag, 1969).

danger, of having gone through an experience all the way to the end, to where no one can go any further. The further one goes, the more private, the more personal, the more singular an experience becomes, and the thing one is making is, finally, the necessary, irrepressible, and, as nearly as possible, definitive utterance of this singularity."[12] The poet points out the fundamental loneliness and solitude of the true artist in this journey toward selfhood; so too must a student of architecture and design be prepared for this solitude, if she takes her calling seriously. A creative individual is simultaneously on a journey to an ever-expanding world of experience *and* to the silent solitude of herself.

Our selfhood also defines our relationship to other people, and our awareness of the limits of our knowledge and experience shapes the integrity of our interactions with others. Whenever I meet a colleague who behaves arrogantly, and deliberately wants to give the impression that he knows everything and is certain of his ways, I feel immediately, with certainty, this person does not even know the foundation of understanding: the significance of modesty and humility. He has not permitted the true character of his experiences to condense around his core of his selfhood, or for the "creative doubt" emerging from experience to soften this center of consciousness and eventually mature into wisdom. The more one knows, and the wider one's perspective, the more subtle one's senses and perceptions become, the deeper one's understanding becomes, and the more humble one is bound to become. The more one knows, I propose, the more insecure and the more uncertain one becomes – and understandably and wisely so.

One of the most useless and valueless words in today's professionalist jargon is "expert." Joseph Brodsky – the Russia-born Nobel Laureate poet – expresses his ultimate doubt about the hubris of "expertise" in this way: "A craftsman does not collect expertise, he gathers uncertainties."[13] When someone is named an expert in an interview or a debate, the title most often means that the person has an extremely narrow focus. True knowledge and experience expand the world and widen the horizon; these ways of thinking never narrow down or close the scope of available possibilities. This continuous expansion of possibilities, I propose, is the reason for a necessary, fundamental, and structural uncertainty in our acquisition of knowledge. You might have known something yesterday, but you do not know that so precisely anymore today, not to speak of tomorrow, because your field of experience has widened even in that

12

Rainer Maria Rilke, Letter to Clara Westhoff, op.cit., note 8.

13

Joseph Brodsky, "Less than one", *Less Than One* (New York: Farrar, Straus and Giroux, 1998), 17.

simple passage of time. Recently, for instance, I heard an accomplished physicist and cosmologist confess that as he began his studies decades ago, nearly 50% of the universe was assumed to be known, but today only less than 1% is expected to be known. No wonder cosmologists today predict that there can be an infinite number of universes, and indeed, instead of speaking of a *universe* in singular, they have introduced the notion of the *multiverse*.

As a student and young architect, I thought I knew well what a door is, or what a window is, but now after more than 60 years of practice, thinking, and writing, I do not know with certainty any longer. Each time the task of door or window presents itself, I need to redefine and reinvent these prosaic elements of construction because a window or a door is not a universal given or a standard thing. A window opening to a garden differs from the one opening to the street; a window with a mountain view differs fundamentally from the one that focuses on an apple tree in the orchard. As importantly, a door to a burial chapel has completely different connotations, requirements, and meanings than the one leading to a house or a grain store. Windows and doors, as all deep and authentic images in architecture, have their ontologies and their histories, and even today's generic glass wall needs to remember and dream of the historicity of the window. Meaningful works of architecture and art are not mere momentary images, inventions, or generic constructions. On the contrary, these constructions are condensations of artistic works and ideas across time and specific frameworks for the singular experiences of life. All meaningful works of art and architecture constitute the continuum of tradition.

I emphasize the value of modesty, but I also need to say firmly that only a humility connected with a sense of inner pride can be productive. You must be proud of your curiosity and open-mindedness, as well as your willingness to turn away from conventions and stereotypes. This is not a contradiction, but a necessary complementarity: you must become proud of your sincere humility, acquired through true experiences of life.

Mature selfhood is essentially a dialog with the world, with its historicity, cultures, and other individuals. Selfhood is a verb rather than a noun – an act of becoming rather than a defined or given destination, a desire and a longing rather than an objective condition. Architecture, likewise, is a verb that seeks to facilitate, condition, and mediate. Selfhood is the ground of human relationships and friendships, as a mutual friendship is a relationship of separate, independent, and autonomous selves. Without complete independence, respect, and freedom, friendship turns suppressive. In my view, friendships form our most valuable emotive and mental capital in life. Friends create the human core of our world, and eventually we remember, know, understand, and feel our life-world through the capacities and sensibilities of our circle of intimate friends. True friends travel, read, and think on our behalf. In our solitary moments of work, they are our absent critics and advisors. We should cultivate our individual sense of selfhood by cultivating friendships as extensions of our own sensibilities, interests, and skills. Having a master cabinet maker as a friend demonstrates the skill and meaning of the hand and what it takes to make things well. We also learn and internalize the ethics of making through such friends. A skillful bronze caster friend will inevitably teach us the magic and alchemy of matter, a poet friend will concretize the reality of feeling and imagination and the true magic of words, a philosopher friend will teach us to think with clarity and subtlety, and a painter friend will assist us to see and understand the true realities beyond the sensory world.

I understand myself in my core as an educator, as a teacher. But as I use the infinitive verb "to teach," I do not mean verbal or formal teaching. I am speaking of an approach toward teaching another simply but significantly through presence and behavior – a process providing a student the opportunities for unconscious identification and osmosis. I gained this insight from my longtime friend John Hejduk – the legendary dean of the School of Architecture at The Cooper Union in New York – who when asked what his teaching method was, answered "Osmosis, I teach through osmosis."[14] Very simply, we simulate, echo, and absorb the personalities and characteristics of our friends, teachers, and heroes. Here, too, I should emphasize that we all need to have our heroes and models, at any age, across time. In this, I am no different from you.

While it is well-known that couples who have been married for many years begin to resemble and behave like each other, we also simulate and absorb physical environments and situations, natural and constructed, identifying with them, in a sense coming to resemble them in our inner selves. "Paul Cézanne's landscapes make us feel how the world touches us," Merleau-Ponty tells us.[15] Antoine de Saint-Exupery, the legendary early French aviator and poet, makes a stunning suggestion: "We do not see precisely with our eyes, we can see clearly only by our hearts."[16]

14

John Hejduk and David Shapiro, John Hejduk or the architect who drew angels, *Architecture and Urbanism,* 244, 1991, 59.

15

Maurice Merleau-Ponty, Cézanne's Doubt," *Sense and Non-Sense,* (Evanston, Illinois: Northwestern University Press, 1964), 19.

16

Antoine de Saint-Exupery, *Little Prince* (Wordsworth Editions Limited, 1995).

Our friendships can also teach us the artistic virtues – the arts of the heart. I appreciate meeting my friend – the Finnish painter Tor Arne, who is 3 years older than me, because we speak about poetry, music, the ethical sense, and of the true human qualities and virtues. During the 60 years of our friendship, I have designed 11 humble studio projects for him, and he has taught me that the highest qualities in painting are not appearances as much as they are essences with an ethical echo. Our common ground is the belief that great paintings are evidence of how we see and comprehend the authentic aspects of the world. As the social psychiatrist Erich Fromm wrote remarkably in his book *Escape from Freedom*: "Beauty is not the opposite of the ugly, but of the false." [17] The great Russian writer Fyodor Dostoevsky even believed that "beauty will save the world."[18] So do I: only beauty and sensitivity to beauty can save the world, and this is the grand task of the arts.

Magically, we can even make friends with great individuals who may have died decades or centuries before us and ask them cordially to become our mentors. If we are sensitive, perceptive, and brave enough, we may name Piero della Francesca, Johannes Vermeer, or Filippo Brunelleschi our personal teacher. I can say sincerely that Brunelleschi has been one of my teachers since my student years. His noble Foundling Hospital in Florence has been one of the strongest inspirations for me in architecture. The seemingly weightless poising of the architecture's upper volume on the slender columns and graceful vaults of the portico below is an example of true architectural magic.

One of my closest friends was Tapio Wirkkala, the legendary Finnish designer, sculptor, and artist, a true genius of form, who was 21 years my senior. Age is not a factor in a true friendship, and I have had numerous friends both decisively older and younger than myself. Tapio often told me about his true teacher and mentor – Piero della Francesca, who was born in 1416 and died in 1492, 418 years before my friend's birth. This is true friendship and genuine mentorship. We are all historical and evolutionary beings – in fact biologically and genetically we are millions of years old – and we can only be as wise and as good as our friends, those living and those long dead.

I have spoken about the significance of friendships for a person with a creative calling. But that advice would be one-sided without simultaneously emphasizing the meaning of isolation and solitude – a condition to which I referred earlier. Creative work is finally bound to take place in solitude and in inner mental silence. The French

17
Erich Fromm,
source unidentified.

18
Fyodor Dostoyevsky,
source unidentified.

existentialist philosopher and writer Jean-Paul Sartre wrote sitting in the restless activity of the cafés of Paris, but he must have had an exceptional capacity to silence the world around him in his mind and project an encompassing inner silence amid the constant social chatter and clink and clatter of glassware and dishes.

Correspondingly, great art always silences the world around us, and simultaneously our very soul. As I look at one of my favorite paintings – Giorgione's enigmatic *Tempiesta* (The Tempest), in the Accademia Gallery in Venice, the world around me is totally silenced. There may well be hundreds of restless visitors in the museum space, but the painting's aura silences the clamor of the crowd and places me alone with that emotive scene in total silence in contemplating a masterpiece of art in that gallery.

The resonances of Rilke's letters to the young poet are instructive and inspirational in the search for selfhood and can be valued whether in the cause of writing poetry or in the cause of designing architecture. In his first letter to the young poet, Rilke advises: "You ask whether your verses are good [. . .] I beg you to give up all that. You are looking outward, and that above all you should not do now. Nobody can counsel and help you, nobody. There is only one single way. Go into yourself. Search for the reason that bids you write, find out whether it is spreading out its roots in the deepest places of your heart, acknowledge to yourself whether you would have to die if it denied you to write. This above all – ask yourself in the stillest hour of your night: must I write? Delve into yourself for a deep answer. And if this should be affirmative, if you may meet this earnest question with a strong and simple 'I must', then build your life according to this necessity; your life even its most indifferent and slightest hour must be a sign of this urge and testimony to it."[19] In his seventh letter to the young poet, Rilke writes further: "[. . .] It is good to be solitary, for solitude is difficult; that something is difficult must be a reason the more for us to do it."[20] And, lastly in this regard, Rilke adds yet another question in his eighth letter: "Why do you want to shut out of your life any agitation, any pain, any melancholy, since you do not know what these states are working upon you?"[21]

If each time Rilke uses the word "write," we substitute the word "design," the meaning remains the same: instead of seeking external references, characteristics, and qualifications for creative work, search within yourself, your own mental world, your memories, and your dreams. In today's educational approach, this essential inner

19

Rainer Maria Rilke, *Letters to a Young Poet,* transl. by M.D. Herter Norton (New York and London: W. W. Norton & Co., 1993), 18–19.

20

Rainer Maria Rilke, op.cit., 53.

21

Rainer Maria Rilke, op.cit., 70.

world of the student is usually disregarded; together with Rilke, I propose a countering approach – one emphasizing an intensely focused self-awareness. In his tenth and last letter to the younger poet, Rilke finally advises: "The stillness must be immense in which such sounds and movements have room, and when one thinks that to do it all the presence of the far-off sea comes chiming in as well, perhaps as the innermost tone in that prehistoric harmony, then one can only wish for you that you are confidently and patiently letting that lofty solitude work upon you, which is no more to be stricken out of your life [. . .]."[22]

22

Rainer Maria Rilke, op.cit., 76–77.

THE SPACE OF IMAGINATION   2
Emotion, Memory, and the Imagination

Creativity is usually regarded as a quality that arises from independent discovery and the unknown, the unforeseen, and the view into the future. Yet, the creative leap is necessarily always grounded in what is known and what has already been experienced; the future is not a discontinuous leap, but an unavoidable projection of the past. In fact, the true sources for creative images are the deepest and almost forgotten memories stored in our historicity, in our body, and its unconscious memories. As Rilke points out beautifully in *The Notebooks of Malte Laurids Brigge:* "Verses [in poetry] are not, as people imagine, simply feelings. . . they are experiences. For the sake of a single verse, one must see many cities, men, and things, one must know the animals, one must feel how the birds fly and know the gesture with which the little flowers open in the mornings."[1]

Personal experiences and memories are the raw materials of our imaginative thought. The dreams and the products of our imagination are not detached inventions or fabrications; they are projections of our unconscious memory. Even dreams have their origins and "raw materials" – this is exactly what Sigmund Freud studied more than a century ago. In fact, while the publication of Freud's *The Interpretation of Dreams* in 1900[2] signaled the beginning of the century of modernity, the door that he opened into the universe of our unconscious world has all but been forgotten. Many of his views may seem forced and strange to today's readers, particularly the significance given to the child's parental relationships and the role of sexuality in the formation of human character, but the existence and significance of the unconscious realm of the human mind and neural system cannot be denied.[3] We are historical beings.

Also, in the arts and in architecture, the creative process recalls, reinterprets, and reshapes experiences and memories, whether conscious, preconscious, or unconscious. We may be working on a painting, poem, or an architectural design task, but we are

1

Rainer Maria Rilke, *The Notebooks of Malte Laurids Brigge* (New York and London: W.W. Norton & Co., 1992), 26.

2

Sigmund Freud, *The Interpretation of Dreams* (1900) (New York: The Modern Library, 1994).

3

The significance of our unconscious neural system is beyond any doubt. On the basis of the number of synapses and their connections, the Finnish neurologist Matti Bergström has estimated the relative information handling capacity of our conscious and unconscious neural systems; if the capacity of the conscious system is indicated by digit 1, the total capacity is in the range of ten to seventeenth power. Matti Bergström, *Aivot ja evoluutio* (Helsinki: WSOY, 1985).

Rootedness: Reflections for Young Architects. First edition. Juhani Pallasmaa. Edited by Peter MacKeith.
© 2024 John Wiley & Sons Ltd. Published 2024 by John Wiley & Sons Ltd.

unconsciously also working on ourselves, on our constitution as it were, excavating into our forgotten memories and experiences, although we are not usually aware of this activity. The deeper our memories are, the more experiential and emotive power they contain and can release. In a compelling dream description, for example, Freud's protégé, Carl G. Jung, gives an illuminating record of the layered historicity of the human mind and memory and the identification of our identity with the dreamlike, oneiric house. Jung found himself on the upper story of a house, in a salon furnished with fine old rococo furniture. Descending the stairs, he reaches the ground floor where the furnishings are medieval. Behind a heavy door, he discovers a stairway leading down into the cellar. The vaulted cellar apparently dates from Roman times. The floor is made of stone slabs, and one slab is provided with a ring. Lifting the stone slab, he finds a stairway of narrow steps which lead him to a low cave cut into rock. Scattered on the dust-covered floor, like the remains of a primitive culture, are bones and broken pottery.[4]

4

Carl Jung's dream is quoted in *Environmental & Architectural Phenomenology Newsletter*, David Seamon, ed. Vol. 10, No. 2 (Spring 1999).

Even our selfhood – our sense of self and self-identity – are grounded in memory; I am what I remember and the kind of experiences I have compressed into my deep embodied memory. I exist in the material world as flesh, but as my mental self, I exist in my memory, the continuum of consciousness, and my imagination. It is, indeed, a disturbing thought that one day, I might simply forget who I am. I could suddenly lose the immense collection of memories that constitutes my persona and my sense of self as a unique narrative.

Such a loss happens in certain terrifying illnesses. In his book *The Man Who Mistook His Wife for a Hat*,[5] the physician, neurologist, and writer Oliver Sacks describes seemingly unbelievable patient cases in his practice, revealing the complexity and fragility of the human mind, the report on "the man who took his wife for a hat" being just one of the incredible stories of human mental reality. In more literary descriptions, we might lose our self, as it happened to Gregor Samsa – a traveling salesman, in Franz Kafka's famous book *Metamorphosis*, which begins: "As Gregor Samsa awoke one morning from uneasy dreams he found himself transformed in his bed into a gigantic beetle. He was laying on his hard back, as it was armor-plated, and when he lifted his head a little he could see his domelike brown belly divided into stiff arched segments on top of which the bed quilt could hardly keep in position and was about to slide off."[6]

5

Oliver Sacks, *The Man Who Mistook His Wife for a Hat* (London: Pan Macmillan, 2015).

6

Franz Kafka, *Metamorphosis* (Leipzig: Kurt Wolff verlag, 1915).

The beginning – the first step, move, or thought – is always difficult, as the first word or sketch concretizes and determines the territory to come. The opening is always also an act of closing. Kafka's *Metamorphosis* has one of the most dramatic beginnings of a story that I know. In my studies of literary, artistic, and architectural atmospheres, I have been interested in how great writers open their stories and immediately set an enticing atmosphere that continues to guide the reader through the entire novel – in the case of Thomas Mann's *The Magic Mountain*[7] throughout its over 2000 pages, and in the case of Marcel Proust's *In Search of Lost Time*[8] throughout its six volumes. Ernst Hemingway begins his classic novella *The Old Man and the Sea* with an atmospheric first paragraph: "He was an old man who fished alone in a skiff in the Gulf Stream and he had gone eighty-four days now without taking a fish. In the first forty days without a fish the boy's parents had told him that the old man was now definitely and finally *salao*, which is the worst form of unluck, and the boy had gone at their orders in another boat, which caught three good fish the first week."[9] With these few sentences, Hemingway sets a feeling of sad disappointment and hopelessness – a feeling that becomes the integrating atmosphere of the novel.

Alain Robbe-Grillet, a writer of the French experimental group OULIPO, offers a further example of architectural atmosphere in literature, at the beginning of his short story "Jealousy": "Now the shadow of the column – the column that supports the southwest corner of the roof – divides the corresponding corner of the veranda into two equal parts. This veranda is a wide, covered gallery surrounding the house on three sides. Since its width is the same for the central portion as for the sides, the line of shadow cast by the column extends precisely to the corner of the house; but it stops there, for only the veranda flagstones are reached by the sun, which is still high in the sky."[10] The writer even includes a floor plan of the fictitious house in the book, indicating the shadow of the column.

The concept of atmosphere is the integrating medium of a novel as well as of architecture. To introduce the main themes, the overall essence, and then create a continuous and consistent articulation of the entity is also a requirement in architecture. Buildings, too, have their narratives and choreographies.

7
Thomas Mann, *Magic Mountain*, transl. John E. Woods, 1924.

8
Marcel Proust, *In Search of Lost Time*, trans. C.K. Scott Mongrieff and Terence Kilmartin (London: Vintage, 1996).

9
Ernest Hemingway, *The Old Man and the Sea* (Frogmore, St Albans: Triad/Panther Books, 1976).

10
Alain Robbe-Grillet, *Two Novels by Robbe-Grillet: Jealousy and In the Labyrinth* (New York: Grove Press, 1965), 39.

We usually think that memory is purely a cerebral gift, but our entire body remembers. This embodied memory is frequently existentially more significant than the memory that we identify with our brain. In Proust's monumental 3500-page novel, the protagonist (the writer himself) reconstructs the room, in which he fell asleep, on the basis of his body memory: "My body, still too heavy with sleep to move, would endeavor to construe from the pattern of its tiredness the position of its various limbs, in order to deduce therefrom the direction of the wall, the location of the furniture, to piece together and give a name to the house in which it lay. Its memory, the composite memory of its ribs, its knees, its shoulder-blades, offered it a whole series of rooms in which it had at one time or another slept, while the unseen walls, shifting and adapting themselves to the shape of each successive room that it remembered, whirled it in the dark . . . my body would recall from each room in succession the style of the bed, the position of the doors, the angle in which sunlight came in at the window, whether there was a passage outside, what I had in mind when I went to sleep and found there when I awoke."[11]

11

Marcel Proust, op. cit., Volume 1: Swann's Way (London: Random House, 1992), 4.

I must have slept in 2000 hotel rooms in my mobile life during more than 60 years, and if I lie down and close my eyes, I can recall each one of these rooms through my body memory – a capacity that reconstructs the space and its illumination in the manner of Proust's protagonist. This is not initially a visual image, as it is a sensation of my body, but the image can be focused as a visual perception, especially if I imagine myself lying on the bed in the room of my memory and close my eyes. When I cannot sleep after having crossed too many time zones, I do not count sheep – I revisit these memory images of hotel rooms around the world in which I have stayed throughout these 60 years.

Every book we have read, every artwork we have viewed, every piece of music that has touched our hearts, and every building that we have entered, adds a layer in our memory, which constitutes the raw material for both our sense of self as well as our creative capacity. Neuroscientists argue that these experiences are stored in our neural structures as complex interactive patterns, not singular visual images.[9] We continuously experience the world through the ever-thickening sedimentations and stratifications of our experiences.

But these experiences are also the construction materials for our sense of self as well as the image of the world, which we are constructing as mirror images, in the manner of the Borges quote in my first talk of a man drawing the image of the world and, in the end, finding out that during his life he has actually been drawing the image of his own face. Our experiences, travels, the art works we have seen or heard, the books we have read, the buildings we have visited and occupied, and the people we have met constitute the material of memory upon which our later work is grounded, as Rilke suggests. Experiences are also the raw materials for our work as architects, artists, or writers. All this is also construction material for the self. In this context, I remind you of the two years that Le Corbusier traveled around the Mediterranean as a young man in 1911–1912, sketching and measuring what he saw, and how these impulses served as the source and inspiration for his entire life's work. More personally, I recall meeting the Japanese architect Tadao Ando for the first time in 1978 in Helsinki, at which time he told me of his first visit to Helsinki. Ando had long admired the minimalist, cast-concrete Tapiola Church (1965) designed by Aarno Ruusuvuori, but as a young man, he did not have enough money to purchase the bus ticket to the suburban Garden City of Tapiola, 12 kilometers west of the capital center, so he walked this distance along the highway.[12] This poor young man with an enormous curiosity and stamina is now the Japanese master of reduction and condensation, whose works we all have learned to admire.

Memory converts independent and isolated experiences, facts, and incidents into a continuum, creating a unified sense of reality and the world. This sense of reality is crucial for our creative work. The architect Alvar Aalto once confessed: "Realism usually gives me my strongest inspiration."[13] Our imaginative visions are wrought of our internalized experiences and memories. Dreams and visions are a form of an extended reality. On the other hand, "Nothing is more abstract than reality," as Giorgio Morandi – the great Italian painter of metaphysical still lifes has argued.[14] Indeed, his shy still-lifes of bottles, cups, or glasses on a tabletop are images of existence and being of how mysteriously things exist in the world. The sculptor Alberto Giacometti wrote one of the most pertinent sentences on art that I have ever read: "The purpose of art is not to recreate reality, but to create a reality of the same intensity."[15] As architects, designers, and artists, we cannot take reality as something objective and given. Each one of us has his or her own reality, and the process of maturation is the process of gradually constructing one's totally unique world.

12
Tadao Ando in a private conversation with the author in 1978.

13
Alvar Aalto, interviews for the Finnish Television, 1972. *Alvar Aalto in His Own Words*, Göran Schildt, ed. (Helsinki: Otava Publishing, 1997), 274.

14
Giorgio Morandi, as quoted by Vida Katarina Vidovic in *Juhani Pallasmaa: One Week Workshop* (Ljubljana: Faculty of Architecture, 2015), 55.

15
Alberto Giacometti, op.cit.. Origin of the quote unknown.

16

Carl C. Jung, *Man and His Symbols* (New York: Dell Publishing, 1968).

I wish to argue with deep conviction: reality is never what you see and experience. Our sense of reality is a fabrication of our own mind. Yet, poetic and artistic works are not primarily fantasies, dreams, or futuristic predictions, as people (and often also teachers of art and design) tend to think. Rather, they are explorations into the layers and depths of one's experienced reality and memory, both individual and collective, present, historical, and mythical. Creative work is often seen as an exciting exploration into an unknown wilderness, but I suggest that it is closer to an archeological excavation – a digging into the deep soil of one's own being as well as the collective and forgotten memories of culture (those deep, collectively shared images called archetypes by Freud and Jung).[16] The new is always born of what has been, never of a vacuum. This is the essence of Jung's famous dream mentioned earlier. Simply put, the human mind is layered, and it does not exist in a vacuum, as it works on and in the archeology of memory in individual and collective ways. Thus, as Rilke advises us in his letters and writings, it is crucial to enrich constantly our mental capital of experiences and memories.

Creative work is also like hunting or fishing: you never know whether you are going to catch anything at all nor can you see in advance what you are going to catch. If you can see the outcomes in advance, your work will not qualify as a true creative work. Only ideas that have a resonance with one's prior deep experiences and memories can touch us deeply, as Rilke also advises us. Perhaps somewhat surprisingly, we can be moved only by things that we have already encountered previously. A painting, building, or a piece of music moves us deeply because it is familiar and strange at the same time. One of the most intriguing thoughts I have read is by the Catalan philosopher Eugenio D'Ors: "Everything that is outside of tradition is plagiarism."[17] I will not comment on this enigmatic thought further now, as I will speak about the significance of tradition in my sixth reflection, but here the provocation is toward a creativity borne of a sense of what has occurred before.

17

Eugenio d'Ors, quoted in Igor Stravinsky, *Musiikin poetiikka* (Poetics of Music) (Helsinki: Otava Publishing Company, 1968), 59. Stravinsky fails to credit the quote to Eugenio d'Ors. In his memoirs *My Last Breath*, Luis Bunüel also quotes the same sentence and credits it to the Catalan Philosopher.

Memory evokes experiences of time, and the sense of time and duration is mentally as important for us as experiences of spaces, places, objects, and people; we dwell both in place and time, in the experiential continua of space and time. We are usually taught that architecture is the art form of space par excellence, but I wish to argue that it is equally important in all art forms to articulate time for our experiencing and understanding, to reveal the layers and folds of time. As philosopher Karsten Harries writes: "Architecture is not only domesticating space, it is also a deep defense against the terror of time. The language of beauty is essentially the language of timeless reality."[18] Opposite to the common view, the task of architecture is not to create fabricated fiction, but to reinforce and poeticize our experience and sense of the real. It is this fundamental foundation in the real that also gives our dreams their depth, meaning, and freedom. True freedom arises from reality and the acknowledgement of limits within that reality, not dreaming or fantasy. Leonardo da Vinci's well-known observation in this regard remains instructive: "Strength arises from limits and dies in freedom."[19]

The continuum of perception, memory, and imagination gives rise to the experience of reality, and it is emotion that mediates between these three realms. Reality is not a static or given thing; it is our own construction, and we maintain it ourselves; the health and sanity of our minds begin to shake when this construction begins to fail or fall. For an artist or architect, it is significant to realize that all perceptions are not isolated and mechanical sensory fragments, or detached snapshots or episodes. Sensations are always connected to both memory and imagination, and they are compared and judged in relation to what has been, and what can be expected to come of them. To give rise to an experience of reality, a sense of duration and historicity and a distinct directionality are necessary. Reality has always its hidden echoes in the past and the future, and our senses are the instruments to scan that echo.

In my view, imagination is our most precious human quality, likely to be the mental property that most distinctly differentiates us from other forms of life.[20] The gift of our imagination makes us human. Even ethical judgment would be impossible without the capacity of imaginatively projecting the consequences of our alternative choices and deeds. The physicist Arthur Jazonc even argues that, "We could not see light without our inner light,"[21] and here the scientist is not speaking of light as a metaphor, or as a mystical or esoteric experience – he is speaking of the mental counterpart of light. Even light needs to have its echo and representation in our mental imagery. Any stimulus or sensation needs to have its resonance in our nervous system and mind to be grasped and evaluated. Recent research has revealed that we see everything twice: the first stimulus enters our unconscious nervous system outside of conscious recording, and we see consciously only the second wave of impulse that enters the nervous system 20–30 milliseconds after the

18
Karsten Harries, "Building and the Terror of Time", *Perspecta, The Yale Architectural Journal* 15 June 19 (Cambridge, Massachusetts: The MIT Press, 1982).

19
Leonardo da Vinci, as quoted in Igor Stravinsky, *Musiikin poetiikka* (The Poetics of Music) (Helsinki: Otava Publishing Company, 1968), 72.

20
We have taken our position as the unquestioned ruling creature due to our intellectual, communicative and productive skills, but this self-declared position is increasingly questioned through studies of the capacities of animals from mammals to birds and insects. Even the net of communication and collaboration between trees, as well as trees and fungi, make us look at the entire living world differently. See Peter Wohlleben, *Puiden salattu elämä (The Secret Life of Trees)* (Helsinki: Gummerus, 2020) & Edward Kohn, *How Forests Think: Toward an Anthropology beyond the Human* (Berkeley, California, Los Angeles, California, and London: University of California Press, 2013).

21
Arthur Jazonc, *Catching the Light: The Entwined History of Light and Mind* (New York and Oxford: Oxford University Press, 1995), 5.

first unconsciously received impulse. This neurological fact points at the existential significance, or I would say, priority, of the unconscious system of processing information about the world around us. Our sensory mechanisms are proving to be far more complex than classical psychology has taught us. For instance, there is no singular visual image of a moving, shaped and colored object in our system of vision beyond the optical image on the retina. There are three separate neural waves, one for each one of the three attributes separated by 20–30 milliseconds from each other, that constitute the "visual" experience in our brain.[22]

We have two levels of imaginative capacity: fantasy or dreaming, on the one hand, which basically denies and replaces reality, and imagination, on the other, which is a projection, extension, and forecast of the mental and experiential reality. As designers, we need the latter gift, the capacity of imagination – the expanded reality. Imagination basically operates with the rules of reality, not timelessness or zero gravity.

A significant aspect of our imagination is empathy – the capacity to imagine how different situations are encountered experientially and emotionally by others. We tend to associate empathy only with human consciousness, but recent research has revealed that many animal species also have the capacity of empathic feeling.[23] Empathy is a projected emotion, and the empathetic imagination is the imaginative skill that we need as architects, designers, and artists, as we are conceiving environments, objects, and poetic metaphors for other individuals to experience. Empathetic imagination is the ability to intuit the other person's reactions, experiences, feelings, and moods. With our empathetic skill, we step outside of ourselves and toward others. Empathy also enables us to imagine human actions, activities, and reactions; we could hardly even dance with another person without our empathetic capacity. In dance, I must pair myself with the other in empathetic choreography and response. We can imagine how it feels to touch an object or a person, but in our design work, we need to project the feeling of an imagined space or situation and its entire atmosphere and feeling as an experience of another person. We must imagine and mentally experience the impact of place as it will be experienced by another. This is a kind of externalized or projected emotion. A composer and a conductor have the capacity to imagine and sense how the complex orchestral piece sounds and feels; similarly, an architect needs to intuit how a complex building feels through its many spaces, surfaces, and

22

Semir Zeki, *Inner Vision: An Exploration of Art and the Brain* (New York and Oxford: Oxford University Press, 1999), 66.

23

Frans de Waal, *The Age of Empathy: Lessons for a Kinder Society* (New York: Harmony Books, 2009).

details, how it is experienced in time, and how it guides our actions and moods. This is an imaginative task far above the mere imagining of a nonexistent physical object. Empathy (*Einfühlung* as it was brought forward first in German) emerged as a seminal notion in the psychological literature of the late nineteenth century, but as a key concept in art and architecture – it has largely been forgotten during the entire era of modernity. The notion of empathy has now re-entered architectural discourse after a neglect that has lasted over a century. Atmosphere, ambience, and mood are concepts related to our empathic capacity, all of which have also been neglected in the modern era.

During the past several decades, the discovery of mirror neurons as a biological concept has provided a scientific, empirical ground for the understanding of this curious but utterly crucial capacity, upon which are grounded human relations, social behavior, and art. Mirror neurons were discovered at the University of Parma by the research team of Giaccomo Rizzolati and Vittorio Gallese; the two Italian scientists were testing the brain reactions of monkeys through fMRI imaging. The monkeys had been given bananas in alternating fashion, and while researchers had their instruments still plugged into the head of a monkey that had been tested earlier – i.e. the banana was no longer available to this animal – the monkey was observing from a distance the other animal being tested. Unexpectedly, the same patterns of neural activity took place in its brain. What this observation meant was that the first monkey was able to simulate in its brain the experience of the animal reaching for the fruit. The researchers immediately applied the test to humans, and the result was the same: as observers of an action, we have the same nervous reaction as if we were performing the activity ourselves. Undoubtedly, we internalize similar qualities of physical spaces, forms, and spatial atmospheres, but this projective and imaginative capacity probably has a different neural base. Simply said, we create a neural echo of our world in our neural system – an echo that projects existential meaning into those worldly experiences.

The "mirroring" and empathic capacities are crucial for an architect and designer, as we design and build environments for other people – environments for living, working, learning, and devotion – and each case demands different sensory and emotional conditions and experiential requirements. I have often recommended that empathy should be taught or rehearsed in architecture schools, but I do not know of any school that has yet placed this into their official curriculum. As I noted earlier, even animals have been found to have empathic skills, but in the education of architects, this mental capacity is rarely discussed. On the contrary, arrogance and self-centeredness have become accepted behaviors among the designer professions. We rehearse drawing, modeling, and writing, and we practice and exercise sports and other physically expressive skills, such as dancing – why we shouldn't train the mental capacity of empathy that reflects the experiences, feelings, and emotions of the occupants and users of our spaces? A medical doctor, a priest, and a psychiatrist also need empathy, as they are also required to feel on behalf of their patients and congregants. Why we shouldn't also exercise our imaginations? We know now that any skill – that of a tennis player, juggler, violinist, or a pickpocket – takes about 10,000 hours of training in order to develop the necessary neural connections and circuits for the task. A total of 10,000 hours sounds like eternity, but in fact, such an eternity is roughly 3 hours of training every single day during a 10-year period.

In my view, an architect or designer cannot design directly for another person, as we cannot directly concretize or simulate the feelings of someone outside of ourselves; we can only reflect those feelings through our empathic imagination. We can do so by projecting ourselves into the being and situation of that other person. We must internalize the other person, whether we think of them as the client or as the unknown user of the space, and then design intensely for ourselves as if we are that other person, as a surrogate for the future user, and in the end of the process, we give the work as a gift to the other person. Unknowingly, an architect must also be an actor, to act the life, intentions, and desires in the role of the client, or the role of the unknown dweller – of "the little person,"[24] as Alvar Aalto used to call the anonymous user of a designed space. We need to internalize the unknown little person. This is how our human imagination works in design work.

24
Alvar Aalto used this notion often, for example Alvar Aalto, "*Art and Technology*". Göran Schildt (Helsinki: Otava Publishing Company, Ltd., 1997), 176.

Aulis Blomstedt, my professor and mentor at the Helsinki University of Technology in the early 1960s, used to say that the capacity to imagine human situations is more valuable for an architect than the talent of fantasizing spaces. This simple thought became the core of my thinking about architecture, and I have always worked to hand this wisdom to my students. As architects, we need to train our capacity to intuit and sense the experiential and mental realities that our designs evoke, instead of focusing on their formal and physical appearances or their external visual and compositional esthetics. I

THE SPACE OF IMAGINATION

am not denying the importance of esthetic interest and sensitivity at all, but the esthetic judgment cannot be only a matter of applied beautification, as true esthetic qualities arise from and articulate the essences of things.

In addition to artistic training, an essential way of refining and tuning one's sense of truth and beauty is to be immersed in the arts and literature. Reading good books is a superb exercise for both the imagination and the empathic heart. As we read, we imagine the scenes, the human characters, events, acts, and even the moods and emotions of the depicted persons, as these are projected and guided by the author. The capacity of our literary imagination is almost beyond belief. When reading a novel, we continuously construct scenes, buildings, and entire cities in our minds, and these feel as real as if we were there ourselves. Our imagination is powerful enough to cast each of us right into the middle of events, whether an intimate love affair or an epic scene of war. In nearly 60 years, I have made two dozen trips to St. Petersburg in Russia – one of the most impressively designed cities in history, but each time I have walked on the streets of the city, I tend to think of the depictions of the city in Dostoevsky's *Crime and Punishment*, a book written in 1866.[25] At my first reading of the book, I mentally constructed the dark room in which Raskolnikov commits his shocking double murder, and that image still persists in my mind 50 years later. For me, that early mental construction of St. Petersburg by Dostoyevsky is emotionally stronger than walking in the actual streets of St. Petersburg.

Elaine Scarry describes the processes of literary imagination in her book *Dreaming by the Book*.[26] She explains the vividness of a profound literary text: "In order to achieve the 'vivacity' of the material world, the verbal arts must somehow also imitate its 'persistence' and, most crucially, its quality of 'givenness.' It seems almost certainly the case that it is the 'instructional' character of the verbal arts that fulfills this mimetic requirement for 'givenness'."[27] I have recently written about "the veracity of reality," referring to the simultaneous multisensory experience of place or situation. I suggest that an architect needs the same skill in creating vividness, givenness, and persistence in their built images. True architectural quality is similarly grounded in an underlying sense of truth, reality, and the authority of the real. Contemporary buildings frequently appear too strained, formal, and artificial to echo the experiential reality in which they are placed; they lack the "givenness" of reality.

25
Fyodor Dostoyevski, *Crime and Punishment* (New York: Random House, 2017).

26
Elaine Scarry, *Dreaming by the Book* (Princeton, NY: Princeton University Press, 2001).

27
Op.cit., 30

28

Bohumil Hrabal, *Too Loud a Solitude* (San Diego, California, New York, and London: Harcourt, 1990), 1.

29

Joseph Brodsky, "An Immodest Proposal", *On Grief and Reason* (New York: Farrar, Straus and Giroux, 1997), 206.

30

Karsten Harries, *The Ethical Function of Architecture* (Cambridge, Massachusetts: MIT Press, 1996).

The Czech writer Bohumil Hrabal evokes the tangible and embodied nature of our literary imagination: "When I read, I don't really read: I pop a beautiful sentence in my mouth and suck it like liqueur, until the thought dissolves in me like alcohol, infusing my brain and heart, and coursing on through the veins to the root of each blood vessel."[28] A building that is capable of moving our emotions also needs to penetrate into the root of every blood vessel. A powerful piece of architecture is not only seen, but it also becomes part of us, and is felt throughout our entire body. A great architectural space does not only move us, but it also educates and changes us. Joseph Brodsky suggests that the demand of a poem on its reader is "Be like me," and the same applies to architecture.[29] Neuroscience has confirmed that physical spaces and places change our neural structures. Rilke's claim that art implies the transformation of the world and an endless modification toward the good, quoted in my first reflection, must be extended to the realm of architecture. Indeed, this ethical dimension or "function" is the subject matter of *The Ethical Function of Architecture* by the philosopher Karsten Harries.[30]

An architectural imagination also calls for a deepened sense of materiality, gravity, and reality, not for an air of entertainment and fantasy. Architecture is not only technology, science, and rational reasoning; architecture is fundamentally also alchemy, returning to the original mysteries and myths of things. Just think of the works of the greatest of architects – the mythological world of Le Corbusier, the geometric labyrinths of Louis Kahn, or the alchemical magic of the houses of Louis Barragan's. We need to cultivate and integrate our material, empathic, and existential imaginations, not just our formal imagination. We need to cultivate all these imaginative skills and capacities together to fully constitute our sense of reality.

I conclude my second reflection by way of an amazing imaginative capacity – the musical imagination of the composer Wolfgang Amadeus Mozart. In a rare letter, Mozart writes about his process of composing a musical piece: "I spread it [the composition] out broader and clearer, and at last it gets almost finished in my head, even when it is a long piece, so that I can see the whole of it at a single glance in my mind, as if it were a beautiful painting or a handsome human being; in which way I do not hear it in my imagination at all as a succession – that way it must come later – but all at once, as it were. It is a rare feast! All the inventing and making goes on in me as in a beautiful dream. But the best of all is the hearing of it all at once."[31] Try to imagine hearing the entire *Magic Flute* or *Requiem* all at once – an entire musical composition compressed into a singular volume of sound! Think of this as a designer: if one really wishes to master the art of architecture, one needs likewise to be able to visualize, touch, and feel the complexities of an architectural work as a singular synthetic experience – an overall atmosphere – all at once.

31
A letter of Wolfgang Amadeus Mozart, as quoted in Anton Ehrenzweig, *The Psychoanalysis of Artistic Vision and Hearing: An Introduction to a Theory of Unconscious Perception* (London: Sheldon Press, 1975), 107–108.

On my daily four-kilometer walk to primary school in Central Finland as a young boy, always alone, through forests and fields, I often stopped at the always open doorway of the otherworldly village smithy near the school to have a glimpse of the shamanic image of the blacksmith. The door was open even in the shivering mid-winter cold because of the heat produced by the forge in the pitch-black room. The smith's huge hands, blackened by grease and soot (The whole man appeared to have been cast of iron.), seemed capable of holding a piece of glowing iron directly and molding the molten metal into the desired form by his fingers. The smith, who could make horseshoes, hinges, nails, knives, and scythes, represented the ultimate human skills in my boy's imagination; the smith was not only a craftsman for me, but he was also a magician and a demigod. In fact, in the mythologies of both the Finnish national epic *The Kalevala*[1] and the African culture of the Dogon tribe of Mali,[1] the smith is a hero possessing and mediating secret knowledge. The smith in the *Kalevala* forged for his people a device called *sampo*, one that brought endless wealth, whereas the mythical smith of the Dogon descended from the skies on a device that continues to this day to be the model for their houses, and the key to their mythology and taxonomy of the world.[2]

As a young boy, I also admired the multiple manual skills of my farmer grandfather. I remember having compared his short, thick, and strong fingers, fit to use farming and forestry tools and the primitive machinery of the time, with the long and thin fingers of my auditor father who worked with a sharp pen and paper and a mysterious mechanical calculating machine, another piece of secret and futuristic knowledge for my little boy's mind. I realized early on that a person's trade and character could be read in his hands.

I still feel emotionally attached to individuals who work with their hands and bodies. Devoted and skillful work always moves me, and

1

Elias Lönnrot, *Kalevala: The Epic of the Finnish People*, Transl., Eino Friberg, ed. (Kustannusosakeyhtio Otava, 1989).

2

Marcel Griaule, *Conversations with Ogotemmeli: An Introduction to Dogon Religious Ideas* (London: Oxford University Press, 1965).

there is something primordially mythical and deeply touching. I would even say biblical, about a deep devotion to work, especially in the crafts and physical work of traditional societies. The dedication of one's life, body, and skills to a specific task is moving, whether in the performance of a musician or sportsman, cabinetmaker or goldsmith, miner or jeweler. The unity of the maker and their work is a lifelong marriage of sorts. I have often had a tear in my eye when looking at the leathery hands of a shoemaker or a mutilated finger of a carpenter; a missing finger or two used to be the sign of nobility in this craft. At my high school age, as I aspired to become a surgeon, I read biographies of famous surgeons, and was both impressed and shocked to learn that some of the masters of early surgery had their little finger cut off in order to enable their hand to penetrate deeper into the surgical cut in the patient's flesh. One needs to make sacrifices for one's devotion; as long as large architectural drawings were drawn by hand on horizontal drafting tables with T-squares and triangles, the architect usually suffered an aching back.

André Wogensky, Le Corbusier's close assistant for some twenty years, describes his master's hands touchingly: "Then I would let my eyes go from his face down to his hands. I would then discover Le Corbusier. It was his hands that revealed him. It was as if his hands betrayed him. They spoke all his feelings, all the vibrations of his inner life that his face tried to conceal. [. . .] Hands that one might have thought Le Corbusier had drawn himself, with that trait made of a thousand small successive traces that seemed to look for one another but that in the end formed a precise and exact line, that unique contour that outlined the shape and defined it in space. Hands that seemed to hesitate but from which precision came. Hands that always thought. Just like he did in his thinking, and on his hands one could read his anxiety, his disappointments, his emotions and his hopes. [. . .] Hands that had drawn, and were to draw, all his work."[3]

3

André Wogenscky, *Le Corbusier's Hands* (Cambridge, Massachusetts: MIT Press, 2006), 6.

I have already given the advice to seek friendships with makers, skilled professionals, craftsmen, artists, and artisans. These friendships will strengthen an aspiring designer's sense of reality and concretize the understanding of materiality, tools, processes, tactility, and forms. Particularly in this age of digitalization and excessive abstraction, contacts with the processes of material making are seminal. These contacts also strengthen one's sense of humility and pride. Having watched a master craftsman work on an object, you do not ever want to give them a drawing of an ugly or poorly conceived object for execution. A beautifully made wood cabinet, a ceramic bowl, or a hammered silver object makes me feel humble and grateful; I do not need to own it, just seeing the skill is enough. The beauty of an object is not the property of its lucky owner alone, it is a gift to all of us.

In my view, as architects we should learn at least one craft well, because not only will that enable us to appreciate what it takes to make things well in any other material or skill, but it will also help us to develop a respect for all other skills of making and for the skilled makers themselves. I have worked as a farm hand, a forest worker, an assistant to a spray gun painter in a furniture factory, a storekeeper in a metal import company, an assistant to bricklayers and tile setters, and I have wheelbarrowed concrete and plaster on construction sites. I have also worked on several construction sites (mainly for the use of my family), and as a draftsman, graphic designer, teacher, and exhibition designer. Additionally, I have worked as a university rector, a professor, and a museum director, and as a writer. I am sincerely grateful for all these experiences, as true understanding can only grow from personal involvement and experience. The separation of work into physical labor and mental work is still common, but I have always objected to such false simplification. All work is always both physical and mental at the same time, and an ethical identification with one's work is crucial in all cases.

Architects used to be in close contact with construction work and with the diverse processes of making. During my early studies in the late 1950s in Finland, six months of practice on a construction site was mandatory. But during the past decades we have become catastrophically distanced from the realities of materials, physical work, and crafts, as well as the skills of the hand and the social atmosphere of construction sites and workshops. We do not know anymore the hardness, weight, and strength of materials or how to work, mold, and join them. We do not know how materials age, and, hardly, how they feel to our touch.

Historically, architectural projects were largely developed in conjunction with the methods and means of construction work itself, not as preconceived and abstracted ideas in drawings. Filippo Brunelleschi, the Renaissance master of Florence, and one of the greatest architects of all time was initially a clockmaker, but he ended up designing immense construction machinery to elevate huge stones to unforeseen heights at the construction site of his Duomo – the largest span of the era in the entire world. This was an era when architects were

still generalists, and highly respected and trusted men in their societies. He also devised a water vehicle, a mechanical water creature of
sorts, to transport stones along the Arno River to his cathedral site.
When the Florentine army was losing their war against the neighboring town of Lucca, the famous architect–inventor was called to
rescue the army of his hometown. The architect had the brilliant
idea to reroute the adjacent river to drown the army of the enemy.
History tells us that the strategy failed, and Brunelleschi himself lost
his bed when the water rushed on the Florentine army instead of
the enemy.[4]

4

Ross King, *Brunelleschi's
Dome* (London: Penguin
Books, 2000), 126.

In the past, architects worked in close collaboration with the construction site and different craftsmen, and their own studios had the
ambience of artists' or artisans' workshops. Today, architects' offices
look sadly like lawyers' offices, and this sight makes me feel a deep
sadness and loss. We should be makers, not assemblers, coordina-
tors, or administrators. The studios of craftsmen and artists, as well
as the laboratories of scientists, are invitations to intense work. With
their tools and machines, these workplaces all have an air of creative
discovery. Studios, ranging from the stage-like study of St. Jerome,
in the middle of an abandoned cathedral, as depicted in Antonella
da Messina's famous painting *St. Jerome in His Study* (1476), to Constantin Brancusi's mythical studio in Paris (now reconstructed next
to the Pompidou Center) with his sculptures in wood, marble, and
sand stone, some completed and some half-finished, collectively
constitute a superb museum of creativity and document the emergence of noble beauty. The studio of Piet Mondrian was as orderly
as a rectangle and as clean as his Neoplasticist paintings of lines and
squares, whereas the studio of Francis Bacon, the forcefully expressive British painter, encrusted with several inches of layered paint,
paper, newspapers, rags, and discarded brushes, sedimented on the
floor, echoed the air of madness in his paintings. This studio resem-
bles a landscape of Bacon's troubled but exuberantly artistic mind.

Craftsmen's workshops have inviting material and tactile qualities;
the smell of wood, sawdust, and resins of wood induce a focused
mood, almost as if incenses for meditation. The soft and plentiful
daylight in a painter's studio makes everything appear clear and
tactile, as if our eyesight had suddenly improved. The materials
of crafts – wood, clay, metals and stones, glass, textiles, and
paper – always look precious and inviting. They are an invitation to
the hand: "Touch me, hold me in your hand, and let me become
something beautiful," these materials seem to suggest. There is an
ethical imperative about material objects of beauty; they are an

invitation to the subtle and sensitive qualities hiding in our own character. Material beauty invites benevolence. Fine work from someone else's hand generates an invitation and an inspiration to work ambitiously and with care.

Creative work of the hand is contagious, and the rhythm of such work invites and energizes others. No wonder work songs were common in earlier days to provide a collective rhythm as a collective intoxicant for work. Intense work also stimulates our competitive instinct; we want to compete primarily against ourselves and our earlier achievements. The work begins to exert its characteristic tune and makes us hum a melody. At the moment when we catch the right rhythm, the work begins to complete itself, and we can enjoy its magical autonomous progression. The master level in any craft, including that of a designer's, allows the work to advance semi-autonomously by its own logic, energy, and will – even a refined building seems to design itself.

This is also the secret of drawing and writing: to lose the self-consciousness and intentionality of our thinking and work, and allow the work to progress through its own energy and inspiration. In this moment, the acts of sketching, writing, and making become automatic and self-productive, and we become a spectator or witness rather than the initiator. In the act of making, our sense of a separate self dissolves: We become our work and the work becomes us. A sculptor's or ceramicist's ultimate clay is, more than metaphorically, his or her own body, life experience, and sense of self and beauty. In the same way, the painter, cabinetmaker, writer, and architect all work ultimately with the given task and on themselves, their sense and identity of self, and their internalized intentions, as much as with external space or matter. In my first reflection, I quoted Ludwig Wittgenstein's assertion that, "Both philosophy and architecture are ways of working on oneself," and this applies to all devoted work.[5]

5
Ludwig Wittgenstein, *Culture and Value*, revised edition, ed. G.H. von Wright (Oxford: Blackwell Publishing, 2002), 24e.

In design schools today, students are often instructed to approach their work conceptually, but I have my doubts about that teaching method. Conceptual ideas and conceptual clarity surely have their role in the design process, but emphasizing the conceptual structure of a project tends to strengthen the conscious intellectual approach, instead of cultivating the emotive, preconceptual, and prereflective poetic imagery and aspiration. I prefer to emphasize metaphor over concept, because a metaphor contains poetic sensory and sensual dimensions, whereas concept is intellectualized and abstracted. I even dislike writing an outline or synopsis for a lecture or an essay, because that obliges me to force a preconception of what I might end up doing, turning the process of writing into mere execution, instead of being a creative process itself. I want to emphasize, however, that this is simply my way of working, and I do not want to press that approach on anyone else.

Gaston Bachelard, the philosopher of science and poetic imagery, writes explicitly: "Between concept and image there is no possibility of synthesis. Nor indeed of filiation."[6] As I have suggested earlier, artistic ideas and works arise fundamentally from images that precede conscious thinking. Constantin Brancusi, one of the finest sculptors of all time whose studio I referred to above, said and wrote very little; but he has a valuable comment on this matter: "Art generates ideas, it doesn't represent them – which means that a true work of art comes into being intuitively, without preconceived motives, because it is the motive and there can be no accounting for it *apriori*."[7] The ideas articulated by the arts are painterly, literary, musical, cinematic, or architectural thoughts conceived and expressed through the inherent medium and artistic logic of the particular art form in a dialectical process with its own traditions and the maker's mental world (I will speak about the role of tradition in my sixth reflection.).

Bachelard divides imagination into two distinct categories: *formal imagination* and *material imagination*.[8] In his view, images of matter are deeper and more emotive than images of form. "One cannot dream profoundly with objects," he writes. "Modernity has been focused on and obsessed with form, but the philosopher of poetic imagery gives primacy to images of substance and matter. To dream profoundly, one must dream with substances," he argues.[9] In another context, he makes the thought-provoking suggestion: "Material is the unconscious of form."[10] Schools of architecture primarily emphasize images of form; but I have intentionally introduced assignments that lead to images of matter, to images and emotions of materials in my teaching.

An emphasis on form also tends to resist and exclude the element of time, whereas an emphasis on material accommodates and expresses duration and time. Alvar Aalto also spoke about the meaning of materials and suggested provocatively that "matter speaks more slowly than form."[11] I have already spoken of an empathic imagination in an earlier talk, and I now suggest a third category of images: the imagery of life, change, emergence, becoming, and evolution.

6

Gaston Bachelard, *On Poetic Imagination and Reverie*, Selected by Colette Gaudin (Dallas, Texas: Spring Publications, 1987), 5.

7

Eric Shanes, ed., *Constantin Brancusi* (New York: Abbeville Press, 1989).

8

Gaston Bachelard, "Introduction", *Water and Dreams: An Essay on the Imagination of Matter* (Dallas, Texas: Dallas Institute, 1988), 1.

9

Gaston Bachelard, op.cit., 27.

10

Gaston Bachelard, op.cit., 50.

11

Göran Schildt, *Näin puhui Alvar Aalto, Helsinki* (Otava: Täyd, 1997).

This category is the one least understood in architectural education and design practice. In contrast, landscape architecture is directly engaged in natural change and growth, and architects engaged in building design should learn dynamic thinking from landscape architecture.

Adrian Stokes, the British painter and art essayist, posits: "In a way, all art originates in the body."[12] This argument about the fundamental presence of the body also seems to apply in other areas of thinking and making. This is, for instance, the seminal message of the book, *Philosophy in the Flesh*, by the philosopher Mark Johnson and the linguist George Lakoff and coworker.[13]

Albert Einstein's famous confession of his visual and muscular thinking is an authoritative confirmation of the suggestion that all thinking has a component of embodiment:

> "Words and language, as they are written or spoken, do not seem to have any role in my thinking mechanism. Psychic entities, which seem to be the elements of thinking, are certain signs, and more or less clear images, which can be voluntarily repeated and recombined. The above elements are, in my case, visual in nature and, some of them, related with muscles. Ordinary words and other signs have to be laboriously sought only in the second phase, when the mentioned associative play has been sufficiently established and can be repeated if desired."[14]

These are words of the legendary physicist genius, believe it or not. Einstein was an unorthodox thinker, and he even praised the value of mystery and the mystical in science and art: "The most beautiful thing we can experience is the mystical. It is the source of all true art and science."[15] I do not believe either that an architect in his design work thinks through words; an architect thinks and feels directly with the essences and media of architecture. Reason and mystery are not exclusive characteristics, as we tend to think; indeed, it could be asserted that the architect works to evoke the mystical and a sense of the transcendent through the most rational and material of means.

Alvar Aalto gives a surprisingly similar description of his working method:

> "The frustration [in the design work], I believe, is the complicated and intense pressure of the fact that architectural design operates with innumerable elements that internally stand in opposition to each other [. . .] All this becomes a maze that cannot be sorted out in rational

12

Adrian Stokes, "Art and the Body", *The Image in Form: Selected Writings of Adrian Stokes*, Richard Wollheim, ed. (New York: Harper & Row, 1972), 122.

13

Mark Johnson and George Lakoff, *Philosophy in the Flesh: The Embodied Mind and its Challenge to Western Thought* (New York: Basic Books, 1999).

14

Albert Einstein, as quoted in Jacques Hadamar, *The Psychology of Invention in the Mathematical Field* (Princeton, New Jersey: Education in Vision Series, 1933).

15

Albert Einstein, as quoted in Richard Dawkins, "Bar Codes in the Stars", *Olafur Eliasson: Your Light House: Works with Light 1991–2004*, Holger Broecher, ed. (Wolfsburg: Hatje Cantz Verlag, 2009), 13 or mechanical manner. The large number of different demands and subproblems form an obstacle that is difficult for the architectural concept to break through. In such cases I work—sometimes totally on instinct—in the following manner [. . .] For a moment I forget all the maze of problems. After having established the atmosphere of the task, and its innumerable demands have been engraved in my subconscious, I begin to draw in a manner rather like that of abstract art. Led only by my instinct I draw, not architectural syntheses, but sometimes even childish compositions, and via this route I eventually arrive at an abstract basis to the main concept, a kind of universal substance with whose help the numerous conflicting subproblems can be brought into harmony."[16]

I find Aalto's notion of "a universal substance" thought-provoking, as it seems to refer to a generative atmosphere or tuning of the work, rather than any specific or concrete formal idea or concept.

Aalto's description presents the act of drawing as a way of luring or attracting ideas rather than recording ideas of ideational or cerebral origins. Here the architect clearly disconnects his focused, intellectual, and rational attention, and permits the unconscious and embodied images, and the independent and autonomous hand to take the lead. This reliance on the unconscious was also the explicit method of the Surrealists in their "automatic writing." During the past few years, I have also gradually grasped the importance of the diffuse and nonmaterial atmosphere in architectural and artistic phenomena.[17] Atmosphere, ambience, or mood is equally essential in urban and landscape design, cinema, theater, music, painting, and literature. I have even suggested that the atmospheric sense could be named our sixth sense.[18]

The creative state of mind calls for a diffuse, peripheral, multisensory and emotionally highly charged "polyphonic" attention, rather than focused intellectuality; but I will engage in these issues in my seventh reflection. For now, I will describe an example of this diffused attentiveness in creative work. During the summer months, I work in a small studio built of wood next to our summer house, situated by a lake; the studio provides me with a narrow horizontal window slit across the wall directly in front of my eyes, an aperture that focuses on the surface of the lake. If my wife happens to ask me after an intense working day whether it had rained that day, I cannot usually tell, because my eyes have been solely focused on my inner mental landscape instead of the world around me. I have been staring at the view outside without seeing anything of it, as my eyes have been turned into the inner mental

16

Alvar Aalto, "Trout and the Mountain Stream" (1947), *Alvar Aalto in his Own Words*, Göran Schildt, ed. (Helsinki: Otava Publishing, 1998), 108.

17

See, for instance Juhani Pallasmaa, "On Atmosphere – Peripheral Perception and Existential Experiences", *Encounters 2: Architectural Essays*, Peter MacKeith ed. (Helsinki: Rakennustieto Publishing, 2012).

18

Juhani Pallasmaa, "The Sixth Sense: The Meaning of Atmosphere and Mood", *AD Architectural Design* (London: John Wiley & Sons, 2016).

imagery of my work. In this mental state, the sense of place and time disappears, and you identify fully with your own existence and the work in front of you, or perhaps, more precisely, with your own bodily and mental interior. Your work and you are one experiential singularity.

Intense thinking is a way of molding one's world in a tactile manner, as if it were sculptor's clay. Here, again the role of the hand is seminal. Martin Heidegger famously compared thinking with cabinetmaking: "Perhaps thinking, too, is just something like building a cabinet, it is a craft, a 'handicraft,' and therefore has special relationship to the hand [. . .] The craft of the hand is richer than we commonly imagine [. . .] The hand's gestures run everywhere through language, in their most perfect purity precisely when man speaks by being silent. Every motion of the hand in every one of its works carries itself through the element of thinking, every bearing of the hand bears itself in the element. All the work of the hand is rooted in thinking."[19]

19
Martin Heidegger, "What Calls for Thinking", *Basic Writings* (New York: Harper & Row, 1977), 357.

The hand is so central in most occupations that these tasks could well be categorized as crafts. I see also architecture more as a craft than a profession. In fact, I am critical and saddened by the ways in which the work of the architect is increasingly turning into a service profession away from the notion of material craft and making. Anton Chekhov, the Russian playwright and master of the short novel, used the Russian word *mastersvo* for both of his occupations: medical doctor and writer. Jorge Luis Borges, the Argentine poet, likewise considered writing as a craft, and this attitude is reflected in the very title of his Charles Eliot Norton lectures at Harvard University in 1967–1968, published later in book form as *This Craft of Verse*.[20] These examples suggest that the division of human work into intellectual, physical, and manual work is arbitrary, as all work integrates the entire person. I closed the design activities of my office in 2011, and ever since I have only been writing, lecturing, and teaching; but, I feel deeply that I am continuing in exactly the same craft of architecture, suspended between material and mental realities.

20
Jorge Luis Borges, *This Craft of Verse* (Cambridge, Massachusetts: Harvard University Press, 2000).

Hands are generic organs characteristic of *Homo sapiens*, but at the same time they have a unique individuality. Our hands have a curious semi-independence, sometimes appearing as our companions rather than as a part of ourself. In fact, our identities are almost as much in our hands as in our faces. Hands can give rise to epic narratives, as our companion Rilke writes in his book on Auguste Rodin:

> "There are hands that walk, hands that sleep, and hands that wake, criminal hands weighted with the past, and hands that are tired and want nothing more, hands that lie down in a corner, like sick animals who know no one can help them. But then hands are a complicated organism, a delta in which life from the most distant sources flows together, surging into the great current of action. Hands have their stories; they even have their own particular beauty. We grant them the right to have their own development, their own wishes, feelings, moods, and occupations."[21]

21
Rainer Maria Rilke, *Auguste Rodin* (New York: Archipelago Books, 2004), 44.

The poet gives our hands such an independence and identity that they appear as our true twins rather than mere grasping limbs. In Rilke's text, the modeled figural works of Rodin appear as material writing of the hand – an activity that is able to sketch even the tiniest movements of the skin and its tactile meanings – and to create an epic story in the simple, and apparently clumsy and mute material of clay.

Materiality, tactility, and traces of use and wear enhance the human presence. When touching a door pull, cast in bronze and polished to a sheen by use, we touch the hands of numerous generations. Works of art, craft, and architecture extend the human hand both through space and time. A twenty-five-thousand-year-old cave painting impacts our senses and consciousness with the same immediacy and newness as a Picasso or a David Hockney painting. Indeed, we can imaginatively touch the hands of great artists in history, all the way from the earliest artworks of mankind to the present day, through the encounters with their work. The maker is always present in their work. It is especially meaningful to hold a fine piece of craft or design in one's hand, or to look at a great painting at the closest distance that the museum permits. The object or painting becomes momentarily yours, and it feels so familiar and intimate that you could have made or painted it yourself. As I noted in my introduction, when looking at the "little patch of yellow wall" in Johannes Vermeer's *View of Delft* (1661), which Marcel Proust admiringly writes about, I feel that I am standing behind the painter's back, or, actually, I am myself painting that splendid stroke of orange yellow color.[22] Seeing the cracked black paint of Kasimir Malevich's iconic painting *Black Square* (he painted several variations of this theme during the 1920s) makes one feel the painter's hand and the lump of wet black paint at the tip of the brush. The abstract image turns

22
Marcel Proust, *In Search of Lost Time, Volumes 5 + 6: The Captive, The Fugitive* (London: Random House, 1996), 208.

into an icon that has its roots in the historicity of human experience and thought. When looking at the *Rondadini pietá* (1564) in Castello Sforzesco in Milan, I can feel the passionate and wise, but already feeble hands of Michelangelo carving the stone; he is known to have worked on this very piece six days before his death.

The work of a great architect also invites the imagined presence of the designer's figure and hand as the architectural space, scale, materiality and surfaces are products and projections of the maker's body and hand. We can touch the hands of Michelangelo and Palladio through the tactile details of their buildings; every edge, profile, and indentation is an invitation to the hand, or, rather, to the imaginary hand in our eye. In Frank Lloyd Wright's buildings we can feel the architect's body height and the touch of his hand so sensitive to materials, surfaces, and textures. Touch is the unconsciousness of vision, and it is the tactility concealed in vision that makes objects and details pleasurable for us. Le Corbusier called this quality *la modenature* – the soft rounding of the profile.[23] We experience Michelangelo's buildings and sculptures through our entire body, our skeleton, muscles, joints, and skin. His works are like human bodies in a melancholic tension, and every profile feels like a human muscle or tendon. In Michelangelo's view, as a consequence of the interplay of our bodies and buildings, a thorough knowledge of human anatomy is crucial for an architect.[24] The greater is the work of art or architecture when the body and hand of the maker is always the more present.

The unconscious association with the body and with human skin in architecture makes us feel the surfaces of built structure, and share our body temperature with them. As I entered the great empty outdoor courtyard of the Salk Institute by Louis Kahn in La Jolla, California, for the first time, I was immediately tempted to walk to the nearest wall, cast in smooth concrete, and feel the skin and temperature of the building with my own skin. I learned only later that Kahn's poetic definition for the color and surface of the concrete was "the mat grey of the wings of a moth."[25]

As we experience a work of art, we essentially recreate it through our personal experience. This is the crucial message of John Dewey's book *Art as Experience,* to which I referred earlier and which I emphasize here again: "By common consent, the Parthenon is a great work of art. Yet, it has aesthetic standing only as the work becomes an experience for a human being [. . .] Art is always the product in

23

Le Corbusier, *Towards a New Architecture* (London: The Architectural Press, 1959).

24

As quoted in Matteo Marangoni, *The Art of Seeing Art* (Shelley Castle, 1951), 248.

25

Shari G. Grant, "The sublime void", *Kahn's Salk. A book of impressions of the Salk* (Bel Mar, California: Architectural Presence, 2019).

26

John Dewey, *Art as Experience* (New York: Putnam's, 1934), 4.

experience of an interaction of human beings with their environment."[26] This is the great human gift of art; we can collaborate with the greatest minds of humankind in re-creating the thought and emotion that gave rise to the work. Through art and architecture, we can see and touch through the sensibilities of the greatest artists of all time.

We use the notion of the "hand" thoughtlessly as if its essence were self-evident, and it were merely our mute, submissive, and nameless assistant. But the hand has a decisive role in our entire humanity. Frank R. Wilson, neurologist and writer, argues significantly: "Bodily movement and brain activity are functionally interdependent, and their synergy is so powerfully formulated that no single science or discipline can independently explain human skill or behavior [. . .] The hand is so widely represented in the brain, the hand's neurological and biomechanical elements are so prone to spontaneous interaction and reorganization, and the motivations and efforts that give rise to individual use of the hand are so deeply and widely rooted, that we must admit we are trying to explain a basic imperative of human life."[27]

27

Frank R. Wilson, *The Hand: How its Use Shapes the Brain, Language and Human Culture* (New York: Pantheon Books, 1998), 10.

Wilson regards the hand even beyond its physiological and neurological significances as an essential constituent of the story of human intelligence and its gradual evolution: "Any theory of human intelligence which ignores the interdependence of hand and brain function, the historic origins of that relationship, the impact of that history on developmental dynamics in modern humans, is grossly misleading and sterile."[28] I would like to add that any view that misses our essential embodied essence, or the role of the body in human identity, action, and thought, is equally sterile. We usually think that our hands merely deal with the concrete, material world; but some scholars attribute to the hand a significant role even in the emergence of symbolic thought and language.[29] According to current neurological thinking, even language originates in the hand and its gestures.[30] In our everyday conversations, the hand still wants to gesture and thus reminds us of its primordial role in human communication. At the same time that hand gestures articulate and emphasize spoken words, they are also a relic of the originating role of the hand in the emergence of speech.

28

Frank R. Wilson, op.cit., 7.

29

See, Juhani Pallasmaa, *The Thinking Hand: Existential and Embodied Wisdom in Architecture* (London: John Wiley & Sons, 2009).

30

Op.cit.

In addition to the tangible tool, a skilled practice of craft and drawing combines imagination with the hand: every practice of making calls for a determined intentionality and an imagined vision of the completed task or object. The maker envisions the object to be made early on, and the working process approaches this both deliberately and dynamically. Richard Sennett, the sociologist, makes two basic arguments about the interaction of the bodily actions of the hand and imagination: "First, that all skills, even the most abstract, begin as bodily practices; second, that technical understanding develops through the powers of imagination. The first argument focuses on knowledge gained in the hand through touch and movement. The argument about imagination begins by exploring language that attempts to direct and guide bodily skills."[31] Sennett's argument here condenses my views of the role of the hand in our shared humanity.

The craftsman/draftsman needs to develop specific relationships between thought and making, hand and thought, idea and execution, form and material, action and matter, learning and performance, self-identity and work, and pride and humility. The maker embodies the tool or instrument, internalizes the nature of the material being used, and eventually turns themselves into the drawing or product, either material or immaterial. John Berger, the British novelist, poet and artist, points out this identification or fusion of the maker and their product in the craft of drawing: "Each confirmation or denial brings you closer to the object, until finally you are, as it were, inside it: the contours you have drawn no longer marking the edge of what you have seen, but the edge of what you have become."[32] Here again, the fusion and identification of the artist/maker and their work is emphasized.

A mature designer or architect is not focused on the lines of the drawing, as they are envisioning the object itself, and in their mind holding it in their hand or occupying the space being designed. While working on a drawing, one concretely touches all the edges and surfaces of the designed object by the tip of the pencil, which has become an extension of one's fingertips, as well as the designer's inner mental world. Drawing establishes a connection between the world and the mind. The hand–eye–mind connection in drawing is natural and fluent as if the pencil were a bridge that mediates between two realities, and the focus can constantly be shifted back and forth between the physical drawing and the imaginary object in the mental space that the drawing depicts.

Sketching and drawing are spatial and haptic exercises that fuse the external reality of space and matter, and the internal reality of perception, thought, and mental imagery, into a singular dialectic

31

Richard Sennett, *The Craftsman* (New Haven and London: Yale University Press, 2008), 35.

32

John Berger, *Berger on Drawing*, Jim Savage, ed. (Cork: Occasional Press, 2007), 3.

entity. As I sketch a contour of an object, human figure, or landscape, I actually touch and feel the subject of my attention, and unconsciously sense and internalize its character. In addition to the mere correspondence of the visually observed and depicted outline, I also mimic the line rhythm with my muscles, and eventually the image becomes recorded in my muscular memory, too. In fact, every act of sketching and drawing produces four different sets of images or recordings: the perceived image of the object of drawing itself, the drawing that appears on the paper, the visual image recorded in the cerebral memory, and the muscular memory of the act of drawing itself. All the four images are not mere momentary snapshots, as they are recordings of a temporal process of successive perception, measuring, evaluation, correction, and re-evaluation. A drawing is an image that compresses an entire process, and it also fuses a distinct duration into an image. A sketch is in fact a temporal image – a piece of cinematic action recorded in graphic form. The film *The Mystery of Picasso* (1958) by the French film director Henry-Georges Clouzot, shot from the reverse side of the canvas on which Picasso is drawing and painting with inks and colors, which immediately appear on the reverse side, is a memorable recording of the temporal and cinematic process of drawing. In the case of Picasso, the image keeps changing constantly as the artist keeps taking an entirely new point of departure. The process is a real firework of imagination.

This multiple nature of the sketch, its layered exposure, as it were, makes me remember vividly each one of the hundreds of scenes that I have sketched during my travels around the world, whereas I can hardly recall exactly any of the places that I have photographed, because of the weaker embodied recording in my memory. This argument does not intend to reduce the value of the photograph as an art form in its own right but to underline the corporeal limitations of photography as an act of recording experiences of the maker themselves as compared with drawing.

In the last decades of the nineteenth century, at the time that photography emerged as the technique of recording and interpreting the physical and biological world, the scientist Santiago Ramón y Cajal (often named as the father of modern neurobiology) insisted that all his students take lessons in watercolor painting and reasoned: "If our study is concerned with an object related to anatomy or natural history, etc., observations will be accompanied by sketching, for, aside from other advantages, the act of depicting something disciplines and strengthens the attention, obliging us to cover the whole of the phenomenon studied and preventing, therefore, details from escaping our attention which are frequently unnoticed in ordinary observation [. . .] without the art of drawing, natural history and anatomy would have been impossible. It is not without reason that all great observers are skillful in sketching."[33] This experienced reasoning of an early neurobiologist applies exactly to the value of sketching as a means of observing, recording, and understanding architecture. In an architect's or designer's work repeated sketching of the place or object helps in concretizing the imagined entity in one's mind; the successive sketches are a way of gradually constructing the image increasingly concretely and precisely in one's imagination.

Drawing is a process of observation and expression, receiving and giving. It is always a result of yet another kind of double perspective; a drawing looks simultaneously outwards and inwards – outwards to the observed or imagined world, and inwards into the draftsman's own persona and mental world. Each sketch and drawing contains a part of the maker and their mental world, at the same time that it represents an object or vista in the real world, or in the realm of the imagination. Every drawing is also an excavation into the artist or architect's past and memory. John Berger describes this seminal merging of the object and the artist: "It is the actual act of drawing that forces the artist to look at the object in front of him, to dissect it in his mind's eye and put it together again; or, if he is drawing from memory, that forces him to dredge his own mind, to discover the content of his own store of past observations."[34]

The act of drawing mingles perception, memory, and one's sense of self and life: A drawing always represents more than its actual subject matter. When sketching an imagined space, or an object being designed, the hand is in a direct and delicate collaboration and interplay with mental imagery. The image arises simultaneously with an internal mental image and the sketch mediated by the hand. It is impossible to know what appeared first – the line on the paper or the thought, or a vague consciousness of an intention. Often the image seems to draw itself independently through the hand.

The initial mental image may emerge as a visual entity, but it can as well be a tactile, muscular, or bodily impression, or a shapeless feeling that the hand conceives in a set of lines projecting a shape

33
Santiago Ramon y Cajal, quoted in William Irwin Thompson, "What am I Doing in Österfärnebo?" *Cornelia Hesse-Honegger: After Chernobyl* (Baden: Verlag Hans Müller, 1992), 16.

34
John Berger, op.cit., 3.

or place. One cannot know whether the image first arose in one's mind and was then recorded by the hand, or whether the image was produced by the hand independently, or it emerged because of a seamless collaboration of the hand and the drawer's mental space. It is often the act of drawing itself – the deep engagement in the act of unconscious and embodied and precognitive thinking through making – that gives rise to an image or an idea. A seamless collaboration between the maker and his work is the ultimate goal of creative effort. The second meaning of the word "to draw" – to pull – points to this essential meaning of the drawing as a means of pulling out, revealing, and concretizing internal mental images and feelings as much as recording an external world. The hand feels the invisible and formless stimulus, pulls it into the world of space and matter, and gives it a shape and meaning. "Everything his eye sees, he fingers," John Berger comments on the tactility of Vincent van Gogh's drawings.[35] This very act of fingering the objects of observation or dreaming, intimate or remote, strengthens the creative process. Even an architect needs to "finger" the shapes, surfaces, and edges of his work, and develop a haptic sensitivity to the material existence of the work.

35
John Berger, op.cit., 16.

Similarly in the act of writing, it is frequently – perhaps even most often – the process of writing itself that gives birth to unexpected ideas, and an especially fluent and inspired mental flow. Paradoxically, it is the process of making that inspires thinking. Many writers report that they prefer writing with a pen or pencil rather than typing. I have a tactile feel for the words that I have written with my hand and pen. My sense of identity and authorship is stronger with these handwritten words than with words that have appeared on the paper or the screen without an analogous tactile experience. It is beyond doubt that the hand has a central role also in writing. Certainly the tactile expressiveness of the hand has a central role in the writing of meaningful letters and literature, but creative writing in the arts is even more engaged with our physical and psychic character: writing poetry and music, for example, are both bodily and existential acts. Charles Tomlinson, the poet, points out the bodily basis in the practice of painting and poetry: "Painting wakes up the hand, draws in your sense of muscular coordination, your sense of the body, if you like. Poetry also, as it pivots on its stresses, as it rides forward over the line-endings, or comes to rest at pauses in the line, poetry also brings the whole man into play and his bodily sense of himself."[36]

36
Charles Tomlinson, "The Poets as Painter", *Poets on Painters*, J.D. McClatchy, ed. (Berkeley, California: University of California Press, 1990), 280.

The muscles of the artist's entire body participate in the physical act of drawing; yet, the act draws its energy from the subject itself. The common understanding of drawing or painting as purely visual endeavors is erroneous. Due to the innate and concrete spatiality of architecture, and its irrefutable embodied and existential essence, a purely visual understanding of this art form is even more grossly misleading. When an artist draws a scene, the hand does not attempt to duplicate or mimic what the eye sees or the mind conceives. Intention, perception, and the work of the hand do not exist as separate entities. The sole act of drawing with its very physicality and materiality is both the means and the end. Drawing is a singular and integrated act in which the hand sees, the eye draws, and the mind touches. "The hands want to see, the eyes want to caress," as J.W. von Goethe remarked.[37]

37
Johann Wolfgang von Goethe, as quoted in "Not Architecture But Evidence That It Exists", *Watercolours*, Lauretta Vinciarelli, ed. (Cambridge, Massachusetts: Harvard Graduate School of Design, 1998), 130.

DEVIL'S PEAK
CAPE TOWN
AUG 23 '98

SHARED IDENTITIES   4
Empathy, Compassion, and Collaboration

"Why is it that architecture and architects, unlike film and filmmakers, are so little interested in people during the design process? Why are they so theoretical, so distant from life in general?" asks the Dutch filmmaker and journalist Jan Vrijman.[1] Contemporary architecture and design have often been accused of emotional coldness, exclusive and restrictive esthetics, and a distance from real life. This criticism suggests that instead of tuning our buildings to the realities of life and human experience, architects have adopted more purely formalist attitudes. In all honesty, don't we usually design our buildings – aren't we conventionally educated to design our buildings – based on functional and esthetic visual criteria, instead of imagining them as resonant settings and backgrounds for situations of lived life, or instead of intuiting the behavioral and mental interactions between spaces and their occupants?

"Let us assume a wall: what takes place behind it?" The French poet Jean Tardieu asks provocatively, but do we architects have the same curiosity for life?[2] Architects often view the moment when residents move into their newly designed home as a moment of esthetic disaster. Yet authentic life leaves fascinating and moving traces. A life's history can be traced in the most minute fragments of a dwelling; Rilke, for instance, describes with staggering force how signs of life are recorded in the remains of a demolished building on the end wall of the neighboring house: "But most unforgettable of all were the walls themselves. The stubborn life of these rooms had not let itself be trampled out. It was still there; it clung to the nails that had been left, it stood on the remaining handbreadth of flooring, it crouched under the corner joints where there was still a little bit of interior. One could see that it was in the paint, which, year by year, it had slowly altered: blue into moldy green, green into grey, and yellow into an old, stale rotting white."[3]

1

Jan Vrijman, "Filmmakers Spacemakers", *The Berlage Papers*, 11 January, 1994.

2

Jean Tardieu, as quoted in Georges Perec, *Tiloja ja avaruuksia* (Espéces d'espaces) (Helsinki: Loki-Kirjat, 1992), 72.

3

Rainer Maria Rilke, *The Notebooks of Malte Laurids Brigge* (New York and London: W. E. Norton & Company, 1992), 47.

The realities of our lives as lived possess their own drama and depth. In the late 1960s an ordinary Manhattan apartment with a secret opening in one of the walls concealed by a one-way mirror was rented to a family, and theater seats were sold behind the wall to watch the daily life of the family unaware of living on stage. Before the age of reality television, watching daily life was so exciting that the tickets were sold out around the clock, until New York police closed the theater "as inhuman."[4]

The weakened sense of life in our contemporary buildings may not only result from a deliberate emotive distance or a formalist rejection of life's complexities and nuances, but also simply because geometric configurations are easier to imagine and formalize than the shapeless and dynamic acts of life taking place in them, or the ephemeral feelings evoked by the spaces. The poet Joseph Brodsky makes a blunt suggestion to this effect: "[The city of memory] is empty because for an imagination it is easier to conjure architecture than human beings."[5]

No doubt, modernism at large – its theory and educational methods as well as the examples of its practice – has focused more on form and esthetic criteria than on the interaction between built form and life, especially our mental lives. Yet architectural form is humanly meaningful only when it is experienced in resonance with life – real, remembered, or imagined. The minimalist architectural style of the past decades has distanced architecture even further from the events and realities of life, as a distinct static emptiness has become fashionable. I need to add, however, that I believe in the value of reduction and condensation myself; but it must be a reduction toward the experiential essentials, not away from them. Constantin Brancusi reminds us of this requirement forcefully: "The work must give immediately, at once, the shock of life, the sensation of breathing."[6] Indeed, every great building projects a sense of life and the presence of human beings, and we feel this sensation of breathing.

In this appeal, I am calling for an architectural thinking that incorporates life in all its practical and mental implications beyond the Vitruvian trinity of "*utilitas, firmitas, venustas.*"[7] Indeed, I wish to add the notion of fully lived "life" to the Vitruvian formula – *utilitas, firmitas, venustas, vita* (life). The formalist, reductive attitude to life within much of contemporary architecture denies its essential spontaneity and "messiness," and tends to transform life itself into a formal and predictable behavior. Yet as John Ruskin concludes: "Imperfection is in some way essential to all that we know of life. It is a sign of life in a mortal body, that is to say, of a state of process

4

This "reality theatre" project was mentioned in an issue of the AD Journal in the late 1960s.

5

Joseph Brodsky, *On Grief and Reason* (New York: Farrar, Straus and Giroux, 1997), 49.

6

Constantin Brancusi and Eric Shanes, *Constantin Brancusi* (New York: Abbeville Press, 1989), 67.

7

Vitruvius Pollio, *Vitruvius: The Ten Books on Architecture* (New York: Dover Publications, 1960), 3.

and change. Nothing that lives is, or can be, rigidly perfect; part of it is decaying, part nascent [. . .] And in all things that live there are certain irregularities and deficiencies, which are not only signs of life but sources of beauty."[8]

The connections between the mind and the physical setting are much more fundamental than we have believed. In the 1960s, psychologists observed that the behavior of a single individual differed more in different settings than the behaviors of different subjects in one and the same setting, and they introduced the notion of "situational personality." Today we know that environments give rise to permanent structural changes in our brain and neural systems. In his 1954 book *Survival through Design,* architect Richard Neutra professed: "Today design may exert a far-reaching influence on the nervous make-up of generations."[9] This intuition of an architect, widely regarded as a quintessential modernist, has now been confirmed by neuroscience. "In planning the environments in which we live, architectural design changes our brain and our behavior," Fred Gage, one of the pioneers in the study of the interactions of architecture and neuroscience, maintains.[10]

Built spaces are not neutral and lifeless stages for human activities. They guide, choreograph, and stimulate actions, interests, and moods, or stifle and prohibit them in the negative case. Build spaces give our everyday experiences of being in the world-specific perceptual frames, and horizons of experience and understanding. Every space, place, and situation is tuned in a specific way, and this tuning projects and promotes experiences of distinct moods and feelings. We live in constant resonance with our world, and architecture mediates, articulates, and maintains that very resonance. Even more significantly, the world constituted by the resonances between our man-made constructions and our minds constitutes a continuum.

Buildings are products of our human imagination. This may seem unsurprising, but we do not usually think of the fact that every human structure has first existed as an intentional mental image. On the one hand, on this basis it is depressing to realize that all the ugliness in our man-made surroundings is a consequence of human intentionality and thought of our imaginations not processes or conditions outside the human mind. There is much work to be done, therefore, in the understanding and cultivation of our imaginative capacity.

In my view, there are two qualitative levels of imagination: one that projects formal and geometric images, and another one that also simulates the actual sensory, emotive, and mental encounter with the

8

John Ruskin as quoted in Gary J. Coates, *Erik Asnussen, Architect* (Stockholm: Byggförlaget, 1977).

9

Richard Neutra, *Survival Through Design* (Oxford: Oxford University Press, 1959), 7.

10

Fred Gage, "Neuroscience and Architecture", theme presentation, Convention Center, San Diego, May 9, 2003, p. 3.

projected material entity. The first type of imagination projects the material object in abstracted isolation, whereas the second type projects the spatial construction as a lived and experienced reality in the human life world. In the first case, the imaginatively projected setting remains as an external image outside of the experiencing and sensing self, whereas, in the latter case, that setting becomes part of the human existential experience as a real encounter with material reality. Importantly, the neurological affinity between what is perceived and what is imagined has been well established in scientific studies; perception and imagining take place in the same areas of the brain.[10]

11

Maurice Merleau-Ponty, "The Intertwining – The Chiasm", *The Visible and the Invisible*, Claude Lefort, ed. (Evanston, Illinois: Northwestern University Press, 1992).

The formal imagination is primarily engaged with topological or geometrical configurations, whereas empathetic imagination evokes embodied and emotive experiences, qualities, and moods. The latter is the authentic reality and task of the designer, and students of architecture and design should be guided to develop their empathetic imaginations. Maurice Merleau-Ponty introduced the evocative notion of "the flesh of the world,"[11] to denote the lived reality in which we exist and dwell, and the empathetic imagination evokes multi-sensory, integrated, and lived experiences in this very flesh. As architects and designers, we need to develop the capacity to imagine this lived reality of the world and to project our buildings into this reality, instead of imagining them in an abstracted, contextless, and lifeless vacuum.

What I have said so far raises an essential question: how can architectural ideas and aspirations, particularly emotive qualities, emerging initially as immaterial feelings of the designer in the design process, be translated and transferred into the actual building, and, finally, mediated to the person experiencing it? This should be one of the central interests in the emerging neuroscience of architecture.[12] The emotions mediated by literature, theater, and cinema are usually stronger than those mediated by buildings due to the reality of the human fates depicted in those art forms. We may well agree that architectural emotions are usually fairly "weak," in the sense that physicists speak of "weak energy," but the power of architectural emotions arises from the fact that they are usually constantly and unconsciously present in our daily lives, and they tune our entire experience of being, although we are not usually aware of it.

12

See, Sarah Robinson and Juhani Pallasmaa, *Mind in Architecture : Neuroscience, Embodiment and the Future of Design* (Cambridge, Massachusetts and London, England: The MIT Press, 2015), complete.

In their relative abstraction and lack of the human figure in their representations, music and architecture are related in their mental approach; but the emotive density of a piece of music can easily make us weep. How can the vague and weakly formalized feelings of architecture be communicated in an equivalently affective way?

Firstly, it seems crucial that the designer masters the entire process of design, construction, and use in order to mediate and material-ize even their most subtle intentions through the constant transi-tions from imagery to feeling, idea to form, and thought to matter, and back again. A talented architect constructs the entire edifice in their imagination; every great building has been built twice: first in the immaterial realm of imagination and then in the material world under laws of physics. In fact, we must acknowledge that every impressive building must have been erected several times, because even a master architect hardly ever executes their first idea, and, consequently, every meaningful built project actually contains a number of successive projects, and imaginative constructions and rejections. Ideally, every profound building has been imaginatively inhabited by its designer, usually long before the actual occupants.

In the poet Paul Valéry's dialogue *Eupalinos, or The Architect,* the nar-rator Phaedrus describes the care with which Eupalinos proceeded in his design process. Phaedrus points out the extreme subtlety required of the architect in transmitting experiential intentions: "He gave a like care to all the sensitive points of the building. You would have thought that it was his own body he was tending [. . .] But all these delicate devices were as nothing compared to those which he employed when he elaborated the emotions and vibrations of the soul of the future beholder of his work."[13] "My temple must move men as they are moved by their beloved," the poet adds further.[14] This is the subtlety and sensuality that tends to disappear in the computerized design pro-cess. I wish to add that there is a distinct sensual and erotic quality in meaningful spatial and architectural experiences, as these experiences are essentially sensuous embraces and caresses. Every great architec-tural space is the architect's embrace; but an architectural space is also simultaneously one's mother's and lover's embrace.[15] We are outsiders in the raw reality of the natural world, but architectural constructions embrace us and transform us into insiders.

The idea of projecting oneself in the process of empathetic imagina-tion evokes yet another crucial question: how does such a mental projection takes place in collective work, such as teamwork in a large design office? In fact, all architectural projects today are bound to be some sort of collaboration. In my view, a collaborative architectural project requires the collective skill, sensitivity, and fused identity of a well-rehearsed musical ensemble to succeed in the demanding and seemingly impossible task of collective imagination. Such a project also requires a shared atmosphere and a charismatic conductor. The collective improvisation foundational to jazz music is an example of collective and simultaneous creativity.

13
Paul Valéry, "Eupalinos, or the Architect", *Dialogues* (New York: Pantheon Books, 1956), 74.

14
Paul Valéry, op.cit., 75.

15
See, Juhani Pallasmaa, "The Eroticism of Space", *Encounters 2* (Helsinki: Rakennustieto Oy, 2012), 60–65.

However, teamwork rarely achieves the intensity and integrity of a work conceived by a single creator. Group work tends to strengthen the rational, conscious, and stylistic aspects of design as the result of a process of communication that tends to lose the subtle emotive and unspoken contents. Could a deeply emotive and subconscious architectural entity, such as Alvar Aalto's Villa Mairea (1938–1939) or Säynätsalo Town Hall (1954), Le Corbusier's Chapel at Ronchamp (1952), the late churches of Sigurd Lewerentz at Björkhagen, Stockholm (1956–1960) and at Klippan in Malmö (1963–1966), or Luis Barragan's Chapel for the Capuchinas Sacramentarias in Mexico City (1958), arise from professionalist team work? Works of such subtlety have to be results of a single, emotive, synthetizing, and empathetic imagination and incubated in a singular personality.

The increasing number of standards, conventions, and regulations, and the uncritical use of computerized information and images, in contemporary architectural design combine to distance the object of design from the natural, internal link with the human psyche and body provided by the eye–hand–body–mind connection of drawing, combined with empathic imagination. These conditions account for a perceptible absence of the quality of *vita* in my expanded Vitruvian criteria. Beyond this primary concern, in relation to excessive computerization in the early phases of design, my second concern is that architectural and artistic meanings are always existential meanings not ideational propositions. That is to say: art articulates experiences of the lived world directly in their existential dimension without conceptual, ideational, or verbal mediation or translation. The fundamental message of art is always: "This is how it feels to be a human being in this world and this particular place." I am not directly linking art and architecture; but, in my sincere view, true architecture needs to have its autonomous poetic dimensions, like the arts, to achieve greatness. How could a mechanized process, however complex and technically refined, brings about existential and poetic meanings? Here, again, I remind you of Rilke's words in my second lecture: poetic meaning arises from experiences, not calculations or algorithms. Aren't even the human figures depicted in computerized renderings mere decorations, like flowers in a vase, instead of being authentic reflections of life – the foundational reality of architecture?

The geometric and formal properties of architecture can usually be rather precisely identified and foreseen through formal imagination, especially by means of using projective technical aids, such as axonometric and perspectival constructions, physical models, or computer drawings and simulations. The lived characteristics – the building as a setting for human activities and interactions as well as emotive encounters – call for a multisensory and empathic imagination. Significantly, the designer does not project the building into their current reality of life; a designer imagines the nonexistent reality of the future building and places themselves there. The designer's imagined scene is not a cinematic projection, as the designer has to place themselves in the scene like an actor in a theatrical reality. The fact that computer renderings usually appear lifeless and emotionless arises from the fact that the process of generating the renderings itself does not contain emotive and empathic components; it is a result of cold projective electronics in mathematicised space, impressively complex and subtle, yet fundamentally emotionally dead.

The capacity of works of art, even completely nonrepresentational forms and colors, as with the Suprematist works of Russian Constructivism, the geometric compositions of the Dutch De Stijl, or the color field paintings of American Abstract Expressionism, to evoke emotional reactions in the perceiver has remained a mystery ever since this nonrepresentational art form emerged more than a century ago. In representational art we attach our emotions to the depicted human events and fates. Abraham's sharpened knife approaching the naked throat of his son Isaac in Caravaggio's *The Sacrifice of Isaac* (1603) makes us feel the threat on our own throat. In the painting we also see the ram that magically appeared to be offered instead of the son. Psychoanalytic theories attempted to explain such mysterious mental and emotional experiences through the idea of unconscious projection of self, or fragments of self, on the perceived object. The recent discovery of mirror neurons and the theoretical suggestions arising from this discovery have opened new interpretations to this enigma. Neuroscience explains this mental phenomenon by means of our inherent neural systems that are specialized for such subconscious imitation or embodied simulation. As Aristotle saw the significance of *mimesis* as the ground of all learning, we are not really dealing with any novel discovery.

All great works of art speak convincingly of the capacity of human empathetic imagination, intuition, and compassion. Joseph Brodsky suggests that great artistic works offer themselves as models of behavioral imitation, anticipating the recent findings in neuroscience. Brodsky also refers to the inherent ethical lessons of great literary works. In his book *Sculpting in Time*, the Russian film director Andrey Tarkovski emphasizes the ethical message in art and insists that art should always attempt to change the world toward the good.[16] What else could true artistic ingenuity be than the capacity to imagine something that no one has yet perceived or experienced, and to bring that vague sensation into the context of our physical and lived reality?

16
Andrey Tarkovski, *Sculpting in Time: Reflection on the Cinema* (London: The Bodley Head, 1986), 110.

Educational philosophies and methods can be blamed of an indifference, or outright hatred or fear of imagination. Imagination has also been a target for religious and political suppression, and control. Imagination is our authentic realm of freedom, and there is plenty of evidence how the imaginative world of mental escape has enabled individuals of cruel imprisonment and torture to survive. Imagination is not a simple and singular phenomenon as the writings of Jean-Paul Sartre, Edward S. Casey, Richard Kearney, and other philosophers have shown. Regardless of these stimulating studies on imagination, its essences and qualities are hardly commonly known, discussed, or taught even in schools of architecture and design. Imagination has been both romanticized and neglected; it has suffered of rejection from these two opposite positions.

Gaston Bachelard also divides imagination into two categories; but he names images of form and images of matter, and he argues that the latter are more poetic and deeper of the two, instead of the formal and experiential categories I suggested previously. I wish to add a third category to the philosopher's pair of imaginative realms – that of images of life. These are images of growth, movement, change, action and becoming, and I venture to argue that the images of life are the least understood of images. In my view, profound architectural images are not nouns; they are verbs. John Dewey already suggested that the mind is a verb.[17] Architectural images are always invitations to action, and they are also promises: The floor invites us to stand up and act, walk, or perhaps even to dance, the window offers us a view outdoors, and the door invites us to enter or exit. The stair invites us to a floor below or above. This choreographed architectural script extends to objects; a chair is an invitation to sit, a bed to lie down or fall asleep, and a fireplace to light up the fire and enjoy the heat and its intimacy, as well as focusing and gathering effect.

Artistic works are always bound to be collaborations simultaneously on several levels. The artistic experience is a collaborative effort of the writer and the reader, the painter and the viewer, the musician and the listener, and the architect and the occupant. As Sartre argues: "It is the joint effort of author and reader which brings upon the scene that concrete and imaginary object which is the work of the mind. There is no art except for and by others."[18] "Great poetry is possible as long as there are great readers," the poet Walt Whitman argues.[19] It is equally evident that there are good buildings only as long as there are good dwellers and occupants, but aren't we, citizens of the obsessively materialist consumer culture, losing our capacity to dwell, and becoming unable to promote architecture as

17
As quoted in Sarah Robinson, "John Dewey and the dialogue between architecture and neuroscience (ARQ Architectural Research Quarterly" (Cambridge: Cambridge University Press, 2015), 3.

18
Jean-Paul Sartre, *Basic Writings*, Stephen Priest, ed. (London and New York: Routledge, 2001), 271.

19
Walt Whitmann as quoted in Joseph Brodsky, *Less Than One* (New York: Farrar, Strausand Giroux, 1997), 179.

a consequence? Aren't we turning into senseless consumers of our own lives? Martin Heidegger pointed out this sad loss of the capacity to dwell of the modern man.[20] The modern man's ideal condition is the journey, not dwelling. Yes, we are turning into travelers and nomads, instead of dwellers. In one of his notes, Ludwig Wittgenstein suggests: "Architecture immortalizes and glorifies something. Hence, there can be no architecture where there is nothing to glorify."[21] Architectural thought arises from given conditions, but it always aspires for an ideal. Hence, the loss of the ideal dimension of life implies the disappearance of architecture.

Architectural works are rarely built by the architect himself alone; buildings arise from the collaborative effort of tens, often hundreds, of individuals, experts, builders, craftsmen, engineers, and investors. But architecture is collaboration also in another and, perhaps, more fundamental sense. Meaningful buildings arise from tradition, and they constitute, articulate, and continue traditions. In his book *The Art of the Novel*, Milan Kundera writes of "the wisdom of the novel,"[22] and he argues that all great writers listen to this wisdom; and, consequently, all great novels are wiser than their writers. No doubt, there is also a wisdom of architecture, and all the profound architects listen to this wisdom in their work. No architect worthy of his craft works alone; he works with the entire history of architecture "in his bones," as T.S. Eliot writes about the tradition-conscious writer.[23] The great gift of tradition is that we can choose our collaborators; we can collaborate with Brunelleschi and Michelangelo, if we are wise and brave enough to do so.

My view of architecture as collaboration certainly takes away some of the glory of architecture as a unique individual invention – a glory that today's cult of the independent creative individual tends to overemphasize. In fact, I dare to suggest that our profession should relearn the art of humility and modesty to replace the air of arrogance and self-centeredness that often prevails in today's artistic and architectural world. "Poetry is a tremendous school of insecurity and uncertainty," Joseph Brodsky writes, continuing: "Poetry—writing it as well as reading it—will teach you humility and rather quickly at that. Especially if you are both writing it and reading it."[24] So will architecture. The art of architecture does not simplify the world into self-evident truths or formulas. On the contrary, great buildings open the mysteries, complexities, and unpredictabilities of the world and human life, but in doing so they provide the true ground for understanding, freedom, and dignity.

20
Martin Heidegger, "Building, Dwelling, Thinking," *Basic Writings*, Martin Heidegger, ed. (New York, Hagerstown, Maryland, San Francisco, California, and London: Harper & Row Publishers, 1977), 319–339.

21
Ludwig Wittgenstein, *Culture and Value*, G.H. von Wright, ed. in collaboration with Heikki Nyman (Oxford: Blackwell, 1998), 74.

22
Milan Kundera, *Romaanin taide* (The Art of the Novel) (Helsinki: WSOY, 1986), 165.

23
T.S. Eliot, "Tradition and Individual Talent," *Selected Essays*, new edition (New York: Harcourt, Brace & World, 1964).

24
Joseph Brodsky, "In Memory of Stephen Spender," *On Grief and Reason* (New York: Farrar, Straus and Giroux, 1995), 473, 475.

Hapticity, Intimacy and the Existential Sense

We tend to regard our senses as biologically given and operating "automatically," but the senses are culturally conditioned and tuned, and to a significant degree, we sense what we are taught and want to sense. Sensitizing the student's perceptions is thus a significant task in all artistic education.

We should all learn to see through our artistic and architectural education, as our guide Rilke did on the advice of the master sculptor Auguste Rodin. As a young poet, Rilke worked for Rodin, and he carefully studied the artist's working process at a close distance, and even attached the sense of smell to the artist's tactile working method: "As for Rodin, he was nearsighted: he had the big bulging eyes of a lecher. When he worked, he had his nose right on the model and on the clay. Did I say nose? A boar's snout, rather, behind which lurked a pair of icy blue pupils. In all his sculpture, what you have is his nose working together with his hand, and sometimes you catch the face emerging from the very middle of the four fingers and the thumb. He tackles the block as a whole. With him everything is compact, massive. It is dough that gives unity. His limbs tend to get in the way."[1]

Rilke wanted to learn to see himself and asked the sculptor for advice. The master advised the young poet to visit the zoo in Paris to learn unbiased seeing, through studying the movements of animals. Rilke visited the zoo several times and finally he wrote in his diary: "At last I am learning to see."[2] The poet wrote his poem "Panther in the Jardin des Plantes" in Paris:

> *His gaze has grown so worn from the passing*
> *Of the bars that it sees nothing anymore.*
> *There seem to be a thousand bars before him*
> *And beyond that thousand nothing of the world.*

[1] William H. Gass, *Reading Rilke: Reflections on the Problems of Translation* (New York: Alfred A. Knopf, 1999), 43.

[2] William Gass, ibid., 36.

The supple motion of his panther's stride,
As he pads through a tightening circle,
Is like the dance of strength around a point
On which an equal eill stands stupefied.

Only rarely is an opening in the eyes
Enabled. Then an image brims
Which slides the quiet tension of the limbs
until the heart, wherein it dies.[3]

3

Op.cit., 43. (Translated from the German by William H. Gass in William H. Gass, *Reading Rilke: Reflections on the Problems of Translation* (New York: Alfred A. Knopf, 1999), 43.)

Aristotle established that we have five senses: vision, hearing, smell, taste, and touch. He also suggested the hierarchy of the senses, vision being the most significant and touch the lowest of the senses. This view, which has prevailed for over 2300 years now, has been reinforced by the fact that there is a separate and visible organ for each one of the five senses. However, the identification, number, and relative importance of the senses can be, and should be, disputed. Steinerian philosophy, for instance, based on the philosophy of the Austrian social philosopher and esoteric Rudolf Steiner, classifies 12 senses: touch, life sense, self-movement sense, balance, smell, taste, vision, temperature sense, hearing, language sense, conceptual sense, and ego sense.[4] A study published in *The Sixth Sense Reader*, edited by David Howes, suggests no less than 34 systems of sensing, by which we are related to and interact with the world.[5] Recent research on the multiple functions of our intestinal bacteria has opened another view into the complexities of the mechanisms through which we are interacting with our surroundings. It is an established fact now that we have more bacterial DNA than human DNA, and some researchers even call this newly found bacterial universe our second brain, or even "our first brain," as the early humanoids survived by means of their intestinal bacterial "brain" before the development of the human brain inside the skull, as some of the lower animals still do.[6] However, we do not think of our stomach as a sense organ. Many of the recently discussed sensory modes, such as the existential sense, sense of self, or the experience of atmosphere, are not attached to any specific organ, which has made their identification and acknowledgement difficult.

4

Albert Soesman, *Our Twelve Senses: Wellsprings of the Soul* (Stroud, Glossy-Hawthorne, 1998).

5

David Howes ed. *The Sixth Sense Reader* (Milton Park, Oxfordshire: Routledge, 2009)

6

"Our Second Brain", a French film shown on Finnish television.

Although our current form of culture is totally dominated by vision – "the rainfall of images," to quote Italo Calvino[7] – this has not always been the case in daily life. Historians tell us that in the sixteenth century, hearing and smell were the primary senses, and vision came far behind them. Historian Lucien Febvre testifies for this unexpected difference in the sensory priority: "The sixteenth

7

Italo Calvino, *Six Memos for the Next Millennium* (New York: Vintage Books, 1999), 57.

century did not see first: it heard and smelled, it sniffed the air and caught sound."[8] Philosopher Walter J. Ong argues that the inventions of writing and printing, began to transform the human sensory world toward its current unrivalled visual dominance. "Though words are grounded in oral speech, writing tyrannically locks them into a visual field forever [. . .] a literate person cannot fully recover a sense of what the world is to purely oral people," Ong argues.[9]

We are usually taught to approach architecture through vision, and it is regarded as a visual art form, but touch – the sensations of the body and the skin – are probably more constitutive for our sense of existence and for experiencing architecture than vision in isolation. In fact, vision itself contains an unconscious hapticity, which is important for the sensing of materiality, insideness, intimacy, nearness, and bodily pleasure. "With vision we touch the sun and the stars," Merlau-Ponty suggests poetically.[10] In my own work, both in design and writing, I regard the sensation of touch, mediated by vision, of seminal importance for the atmosphere of an object, room, building or setting. There is also a distinct tactility in language and words. After his lessons in seeing following Rodin's advice, Rilke introduced the beautiful notion *Dinggedicht*, meaning "thing poem" or "object poem," for his poems that evoke material things and objects. *The Panther* was the first of Rilke's *Dinggedicht* – poems and it appears as a visual sketch of the mighty animal in the despair of his cage. We have a desire to touch, as touching, not vision, is the ultimate proof of reality (as well as of affection), as even our obsessively visual culture believes. The biblical example of the veracity of touch is "Doubting Thomas" – the apostle who did not trust his eyes, and who poked his index finger into the wound of Christ. The event is memorably depicted in Caravaggio's dramatic painting of 1601–1602.

When we close our eyes, or are in total darkness, our vision is blocked; but we continue to sense the presence of the space and the material setting in which we are located. In fact, we keep sensing the shape, materiality, illumination, and even atmosphere of the spaces we occupy through our memory and senses. When I wake up in the darkness of the night, I usually know my location in the world. The continuity of the world is maintained by our body memory and existential sense. We do not exist abstractly, as we are always placed and situated. All the senses are specializations of the originating skin tissue of the fetus. Because of this evolutionary fact, the senses are forms of touching or connecting with, and they are interrelated in an evolutionary sense, and they naturally seek to collaborate with

8

Lucien Febvre, as quoted in Martin Jay, *Downcast Eyes – Denigration of Vision in Twentieth-Century French Thought* (Berkeley, California and Los Angeles, California: University of California Press, 1994), 34.

9

Walter J. Ong, *Orality & Literacy – The Technologizing of the World* (London and New York. Routledge, 1991), 12.

10

As quoted in David Michael Levin, ed., *Modernity and the Hegemony of Vision* (Berkeley, California and Los Angeles, California: University of California Press, 1993).

each other. Even neurobiologically the integration of the senses is seminal: all sensory input interconnects at the brain stem, and how we feel, think, and act involves all the senses.[11] The American light artist James Turrell taught me years ago the surprising fact that our skin, especially behind the knee and elbow bends, has maintained the capacity to distinguish primary colors.[12] We can easily learn to distinguish a few colors by the "vision" of our skin.

Merleau-Ponty convincingly emphasizes the sensory collaboration and simultaneity: "My perception is not a sum of visual, tactile and audible givens: I perceive in a total way with my whole being: I grasp the unique structure of the thing, a unique way of being, which speaks to all my senses at once."[13] This is one of the most important things I can teach you: our senses interact and we experience our existence as a unified experience, not as separate sensory messages. The veracity of our experience and of our sense of reality does not arise from a single sensation, but from integrated multisensory experiences. Defining architecture as a visual art is thus a fundamentally reductive misunderstanding. A meaningful architectural experience always addresses our entire integrated being – our holistic sense of existence. In fact, this is one of the ethical tasks of architecture: to address us as complete, integrated beings. And further, architecture needs to liberate and emancipate our senses instead of forcefully guiding them for any manipulative purposes.

Merleau-Ponty introduced the wonderful phrase "the flesh of the world," which I have already mentioned several times throughout these reflections, but as the concept has become so central in my thinking, here I repeat it again. "My body is made of the same flesh as the world [. . .] this flesh of my body is shared by the world," the philosopher explains.[14] He also writes about "the ontology of the flesh" as the conclusion of his phenomenology of perception. Ontology means the primordial origin of things, and this notion underlines the constitutive importance of the philosopher's idea. In my view, our understanding of how we are related to and in exchange with architecture can be firmly and understandably based on this ontology. We exist in the flesh of the world, as does architecture, and architecture can be regarded as a man-made extension and articulation of that flesh, as well as of our own biological flesh. We extend ourselves into the world and internalize and mirror the world in our bodies and sensory as well as mental worlds. Architecture is the extended flesh of our own making, designed constructions that help to fuse us with our world and dwell in it in a coherent and harmonized manner.

11

Eve A. Edelstein, "Neuroscience and Design: Clinical Neuroscience at the interface of Architecture and Health", lecture at the Neuroscience for Architecture, Urbanism and Design. Summer Intersession Program in the New School for Architecture and Design, San Diego, August 15, 2018. Pallasmaa's lecture notes.

12

James Turrell in a private conversation with the author in conjunction with a conference on . . . in the Virginia Tech, Blacksburg, Virginia in 1999.

13

Maurice Merleau-Ponty, "Film and the New Psychology" *Sense and Non-Sense* (Evanston, Illinois: Northwestern University Press, 1992).

14

Maurice Merleau-Ponty, "The Intertwining – The Chiasm" *The Visible and the Invisible*, Claude Lefort, ed. (Evanston, Illinois: Northwestern University Press, 1992).

Several years ago, I witnessed the amazing power of our embodied sense, the existential sense. At a dinner in Sydney, Australia, I met a French visual artist who had totally lost his eyesight nearly 30 years earlier in a violent attack in New York. Two men had broken into his apartment in Manhattan, robbed and beaten him cruelly, and finally poured paint thinner on his face. The chemical corroded his eyes, and he lost his eyesight immediately and totally. When we met in Sydney, he had just returned from Warsaw, where he had directed a ballet, and after Australia he was on his way to Greenland, totally alone. Amazed, I asked him how he could do such demanding things without eyesight. He answered: "I have no problem; I see with my entire body."[15]

We all see and sense with our entire body, but we do not usually acknowledge it. As architects we need to learn how to sense with our entire body. You will not become a real architect before having learned to see and sense through your body and sense of existence. Permit me to add, seeing is not just an automatic and mechanical reaction, as we see what we want to see and have learned to see. Seeing is a process of selection, evaluation, and interpretation. We really need to learn to see and sense without prejudice. The American minimalist painter Frank Stella has argued that "what you see is what you see."[16] Without the slightest of hesitation, I would say the opposite: what you see is never what you see. Only if you have truly learned to see, you may be able to observe in a critical and unbiased manner. We tend to see what we already know about the object at which we are looking. But in fact, as Robert Irwin, the American installation artist argues, paraphrasing the poet Wallace Stevens, "Seeing is forgetting the name of the thing one sees."[17]

Earlier I quoted the Czech writer Bohumil Hrabal, who says that when reading he does not read, he sucks the words in his mouth, and lets them melt and fuse into his blood like a liquor. When we see intensely, we do not really see either; we touch through our eyes. Vision is essentially the sense of separation and distance, but even our eyes desire to touch and embrace. Vision separates us from the world, but the concealed touch in vision draws us back into a tactile and intimate connection with it.

In their significant book *Metaphors We Live By*, philosopher Mark Johnson and the linguist George Lakoff argue that thinking always involves and engages the body.[18] Our thoughts are related with our body, which exists in the world. The body has its capacities, memories, skills, and wisdom. A great musician, say, a pianist, does not

15

Conversation at a dinner at the House of Glenn Murcutt and Wendy Lewin with Hugues de Montalembert and his wife Lin Utzon.

16

Frank Stella as quoted in: Peter Leech, "Criticism and the Emblems of Art", PN Review 15, vol. 7, number 1.

17

Robert Irwin and Lawrence Weschler, *Seeing Is Forgetting the Name of the Thing One Sees: A Life of Contemporary Artist Robert Irwin* (Oakland, California: University of California Press, 1982), 2.

18

Mark Johnson and George Lakoff, *The Metaphors We Live By* (Chicago: The University of Chicago Press, 1980).

usually remember a complete concerto as a written score; their body and fingers remember, and it is the continuum of the composition that supports the musician's memory. A painter friend of mine who used to be the lead clarinet player in the Finnish Opera Orchestra[19] wrote me recently describing the frustration of memorizing pieces of music after having hurt one of his fingers and having been obliged to play with an altered fingering. Another friend, a well-known actor, has told me that he does not remember his lines by heart in isolation; but as he enters the physical situation on the stage, the lines flow into his mind effortlessly. He once played the role of the narrator in a unique staged version of Italo Calvino's *If on a Winter's Night a Traveller*,[20] and his role was to introduce the 10 acts and settings, and to mediate the transition from one scene to the next. His role contained over 70 pages of text to be memorized and then delivered dramatically – through his entire being. I do not remember buildings that I have visited, or even the ones I have designed myself as visual pictures; I remember them as embodied images. Through entering the buildings in my imagination, I can also generate the visual image, or any detail, when needed. In my third reflection, I already mentioned the hundreds of hotel rooms in my body memory. If you are a talented designer in the middle of the design process, you are not looking at the design as drawings: you are there in the middle of all of it through your entire being. You can design with your eyes closed; you are your building and your building is you.

Having worked in architecture and taught it intensely for 60 years, I dare to suggest that our vision is not the most important sense in architecture. We hear, touch, and smell buildings and sense them through our body. The most crucial sense is our accumulated haptic and existential sense. I have already said this several times previously, but I repeat it because of the importance of this argument. This haptic sense places us in space and maintains our relationship with the world as well as with our work, whatever it may be. Moreover, our sense of being is not directly dependent on vision, as our sense of being continues uninterrupted and unaltered when we close our eyes or awaken from sleep before opening our eyes. All too clearly, the blind and the deaf have their existential sense, and they also experience their "being in the world."

For me, one of the true miracles of existence is that I wake up in the morning as the same person who I was in the previous evening and into the same world that I experienced before I fell asleep. I am not

19

The letter was sent by Tapio Lötjönen, musician and painter in 2018, a few months before he passed away.

20

Italo Calvino, *If on a Winter's Night a Traveller* (Penguin Random House, 2010); The actor friend of mine is Timo Torikka (b. 1958).

really my physical constitution; I am a unique narrative – an evolving story, and so is each one of us. The greatest mysteries that we face are not the exceptional situations of life or our consciousness, but the realities we take for granted. The greatest of mysteries are not found in the invisible, but in the visible. As Giorgio Morandi, the Italian painter of metaphysical still-lifes, writes: "There is nothing more abstract than reality."[21]

21

Giorgio Morandi, source unidentified.

DWELLING IN TIME   6
Tradition, Newness, and Innovation

In its essence, the human mind is a layered, temporal, and historical phenomenon. With this declaration, I can sincerely say in retrospect that I wish I had attended more attentively to the history lessons offered during my studies, instead of needing to study history at my current age. As a student and a young architect, like many in my generation, I was looking forward to the future with optimism and saw coursework in history – even any interest in history at all! – as a burden rather than as an advantage or as sources for design. Due to the trajectory western culture has since taken, and certainly also to my own experiences and thinking, I have changed my attitudes, and I now regard history as a necessary ground for creative potential and wisdom. Indeed, I have come to believe that tradition, "the historical sense" of T.S. Eliot, is also the true source of creativity.

Even today, an interest in the significance of tradition is usually seen as nostalgia and conservatism. Commonplace thinking maintains that traditions should be left to the historians and cultural anthro-pologists, rather than discussed among artists and architects and in their education. The histories of art and architecture have been embedded in varying ways in modern art curricula; but modernism in the arts, in general, has devalued tradition as a subject from which artists and architects should be liberated, not burdened. While I highly value the artistic achievements of the Bauhaus and recognize that the Bauhaus had more qualified teaching staff than any other school in the modern era, the beginning student of art and archi-tecture today may not know that history was not taught at all at the influential Bauhaus School, or that the ahistorical Bauhaus peda-gogy has served as a model for modern art education globally for almost a century now.

In our post-industrial era, obsessed with rationality and progress, our eyes are exclusively fixated on the present and the near future. Dur-ing the past few decades, uniqueness, newness, and invention have

Rootedness: Reflections for Young Architects. First edition. Juhani Pallasmaa. Edited by Peter MacKeith.
© 2024 John Wiley & Sons Ltd. Published 2024 by John Wiley & Sons Ltd.

become the sole criteria for quality in architecture, design, and art. As the understanding and internalization of history is lost in education and society more generally, the coherence and harmony of landscapes and cityscapes and their historical layering is not seen as an objective in architecture anymore. Artistic uniqueness and formal invention have replaced the quest for existential meaning and emotive impact, not to speak of the desire for spiritual dimensions and beauty. Today architecture is increasingly a commercial product and an object of trade, on the one hand, and a unique and autonomous expression of its author's personal values, on the other. The standard buildings of the industrialized and consumerist world today generally appear flat, shallow, and devoid of human narrative and contents; in a cultural sense, they often appear autistic and suffering from a loss of memory.

But here I propose a countering understanding that architecture was born as an art of mediation – a tangibly constructed mediation literally between the realms of the gods and mortals. Architecture's obligation in this role was to address the cosmos and cosmic harmony, not mere utility, efficiency, or even beauty as a purely esthetic quality. We are not generally aware of the anthropological fact that human beings housed their dead long before they began to build shelters for themselves, which reveals the significance of ritual and belief in the very constitution of architecture.[1] As Lewis Mumford writes in *The City in History*, "Mid the uneasy wanderings of palaeolithic man, the dead were first to have permanent dwellings: a cavern, a mound, a mound marked by a cairn, a collective barrow. These were landmarks to which the living probably returned at intervals, to communicate with or placate the ancestral spirits."[2] Even the young Alvar Aalto wrote significantly: "Form is nothing else but a desire for eternal life on earth."[3] The authentic conception of architecture originates in the recognition of human mortality – a far deeper and more challenging condition than the transitory aspirations of contemporary design.

Two exemplary architectures can be offered to substantiate my assertions – the first in contemporary China and the second in Bangladesh – as it entered into the modern world.

Accepting the 2012 Pritzker Architecture Prize in Beijing, the Chinese Laureate Wang Shu (He collaborates with his wife Lu Wenyu.) confessed in his speech that he had begun his career with works in the then fashionable Postmodern and Deconstructionist idioms,

1

Robert Pogue Harrison, *The Dominion of the Dead* (Chicago and London: The University of Chicago Press, 2003).

2

Lewis Mumford, *The City in History: Its Origins, Transformations, and Its Prospects* (New York: Harcourt, Brace & World, 1961), 7.

3

Alvar Aalto, Göran Schildt, and Alvar Aalto, *The Early Years* (New York: Rizzoli International Publications, 1984), 192.

but that he had eventually realized that his country was losing its connection with its own Chinese traditions and cultural identities, traditions among the oldest in the world. After this realization, the architect described, he had devotedly endeavored to rebind his architecture to the long and deep cultural traditions of his country, and it was on this basis that the Pritzker Prize had been awarded to him.[4] This was an unexpectedly outspoken and courageous message in the presence of the highest Chinese officials. I was present at the 2012 event in my role as member of the Pritzker Jury, heard Wang Shu's acceptance speech, and observed its impact on the audience, including the Chinese political leaders. I believe Wang Shu's passionate message underlies the later strong expressions of the Chinese President Xi Jinping and the Mayor of Beijing – both present at the 2012 ceremony – against "imported" architecture and their support for Chinese traditions.

In their works, such as the Xiangshan Campus and the Historical Museum at Ningbo, Wang Shu and Lu Wenyu have designed buildings that deliberately reconnect with the invisible undercurrents of timeless Chinese imagery and traditions. These buildings do not echo any distinct formal attributes of the country's rich architectural past, but they evoke atmospheres, moods, and associations that evoke a depth of time and a groundedness to the work in time and history. This sense of rootedness does not rely on any formal language or direct historical allusion, but the architectural logic itself, its cultural and collective deep structure, as it were, in the same way that languages are based on unconscious deep structures. This architecture also projects comforting and enriching experiences of participation in a meaningful historical continuum.

This sense of cultural continuum and layered time is both a patina and a palpable narrative on the buildings. The architects' repeated use of recycled materials, such as discarded bricks and roof tiles, speaks of inherited crafts, timeless and selfless labor, and a sense of a collective and shared identity, all passed on to coming generations through the architecture. The presence of the life and labor of the previous generations through the recycled materials is respectful and moving, indeed, as if the new building were a collective physical effort of several generations. The repurposed materials concretize the course of time and layering of successive cultural eras. They are also silent witnesses of the human fates and tragedies concealed in history. Almost overwhelmed by these experiences and perceptions, I encountered this architecture with a sense of gratitude.

4

See, Wang Shu's speech at the Pritzker Prize Ceremony in Beijing in 2012.

Visiting Wang Shu's buildings made me recall Louis Kahn's powerful National Assembly Buildings in Dhaka, Bangladesh, designed
and constructed between 1963 and 1974, which also project an
authoritative condensation of traditions, ageless and contemporary,
geometrical and mystical, European, and Islamic and Mughal. This
architecture even echoes the Karnak Temple in Luxor, built in during the Middle Kingdom and continued to the Ptolemaic times. In
fact, Kahn visited Luxor before beginning to work on the National
Assembly, and the sensations of gravity, scale, and materiality in his
Luxor sketches re-emerge in his design in Dhaka. Kahn's buildings
express the layered quality of time itself rather than specific historic
examples. They express a deep and "tactile time," in architectural
resonance with the monumental novel of Marcel Proust, *Remembrance
of Things Past*. Kahn's architecture in Bangladesh succeeds in giving
a proud and optimistic cultural identity to an emergent Islamic state
possessed of ancient traditions and contemporary poverty. This is the
impressive potential of great architecture.

These examples of Kahn and Shu show that a respectful attitude to
traditions does not imply regressive traditionalism but the acknowledgement of the cultural continuum as a source of meaning, inspiration, and emotional grounding. I repeat here the very title of these
collected reflections: rootedness.

The loss of the sense of historicity and evolutionary narrative is
clearly becoming a major concern in numerous countries developing at the accelerated rate of today's aggressive investment strategies, expedient methods of construction, and universal architectural
fashions. Our current culture projects an ecstasy of newness and
nowness, and it believes in change rather than evolution. But is mere
newness a relevant aspiration and criteria for quality in art and architecture? Is a future without its constitutive past even conceivable?
The summation is distressing: as a consequence of the devaluing of
history, the loss of tradition, and the severing of the cultural continuum, our lives are increasingly uprooted, alienated, and without
a sense of existential meaning. The value of continuity and meaning in art and architecture might be a useful binding subtitle to my
presentation here.

Our ultra-materialist and hedonistic consumer culture seems to be
quickly losing its capacity to identify the essences, and values of life
and experience. Experiential and sensory qualities, existential meanings, nuances, and expressive subtleties are replaced by such quantifia-
ble properties as overwhelming size, strangeness, monetary value, and

perceptual shock value of form. Instead of strengthening and clarifying the sense of continuity and evolution, often the imagery of today's celebrated architecture aims deliberately at breaking these tethers to authenticity. In the commercial world, references to tradition often serve manipulative social and economic purposes, rather than genuine experiences of integrity. The uncritical interest in superficial uniqueness and newness inevitably shifts the artistic encounter from a genuine and autonomous experience of the work into a comparative and quasi-rational judgment. Intellectual and commercial speculation replaces emotive sincerity, and genuine experiential quality is replaced by insidious quasi-rational quantitative assessments. The final criteria today for artistic and architectural expression often appears to be of public attention, monetary value, and profit.

Today "newness" is expected to evoke interest and excitement, whereas references to the traditions of the art form in question, not to speak of intentionally attempting to strengthen the continuum of that tradition, are seen as reactionary aims and as a source of boredom. In the 1980s, the Italian Postmodern art critic Germano Celant used such notions as "contemporaryism," "hyper-contemporary," "terror of the contemporary," and "the vertigo of nowness," and referred to "a pathological and conformist anxiety [. . .] that turns the present into an absolute frame of reference, an undisputable truth."[5]

5

Germano Celant, *Unexpressionism – Art Beyond the Contemporary* (New York: Rizzoli International Publications, 1988), 5, 6 and 10.

When thinking of the scenes of art and architecture during the two first decades of the third millennium, we can speak of an accelerating "vertigo of nowness." Paradoxically, when looking at new projects in international architectural journals, I often have a feeling of *deja vu* and boredom. The constant and obsessive search for newness has already become a distinct repetitiousness and monotony; unexpectedly the quest for uniqueness seems to result in sameness, repetition, and boredom. Newness is usually a formal surface quality without a deeper mental echo that could energize the work and its repeated encounter. Formal surface variations are endless, while deep existential meanings are always singular qualities. Forcefully formalist, estheticized architecture lacks deeper existential and cultural meanings, and consequently appears always as variations of the same visual game. The Norwegian philosopher Lars Fr. H. Svendsen points out this paradoxical phenomenon in his book *The Philosophy of Boredom*: "In this objective, something new is always sought to avoid boredom with the old. But as new is sought only because of its newness, everything turns identical, because it lacks all other properties but newness."[6] As a consequence, the ignorant boredom with the old becomes replaced by the ignorant boredom with the new.

6

Lars Fr. H. Svendsen, *Ikävystymisen filosofia* (The Philosophy of Boredom), (Helsinki: Tammi, 2005), 75.

Artistic newness is generally associated with radicality – the new is expected to surpass the previous ideas in quality and effect, and to jettison prevailing conventions. But is there really any identifiable progress in art and architecture, or are we only witnessing constantly changing approaches and reactions to the same fundamental existential questions and motives? What is the quality that makes us experience a 36,000 year-old cave painting in Altamira, Spain, with the same effect and impact as any work of the present day? Hasn't art always been engaged in expressing the human existential condition, attempting to mediate our relationship with the world, the cosmos, the gods, and the mystical? Shouldn't art and architecture be oriented toward the timeless questions of existence rather than toward the appeal of the momentary and the fashionable and providing services to economic interests? Shouldn't architecture seek to embody the deep and permanent essences of human existence, instead of obsessively trying to generate passing experiences of newness? I do not believe that any profound artist is directly interested in newness, or self-expression, for that matter, as art is too seriously engaged in existential issues to be concerned with such passing aspirations. A true artist is interested in essences, not appearances. "No real writer ever tried to be contemporary," the writer Jorge Luis Borges asserts bluntly,[7] and the same surely applies in architecture. What is the contemporary quality in the Pharaonic, Roman, and Mughal architecture of Louis Kahn, or the Aztek, Mayan, and Chinese layers of Jørn Utzon's architecture?

Newness is usually related to extreme individuality and self-expression; but, isn't self-expression another questionable objective in art? Indeed, since the emergence of the modern era, art and architecture have increasingly been seen as areas of self-expression of the author. Significantly, Balthus (Count Balthasar Klossowski de Rola) – one of the finest figurative painters of the late twentieth century – expresses a converse view: "If a work only expresses the person who created it, it wasn't worth doing [. . .] Expressing the world, understanding it, that is what seems interesting to me."[8] Here the painter reinforces the previously cited argument of Merleau-Ponty: "We come not to see the work of art, but the world according to the work." Later, Balthus re-formulated his argument: "Great painting has to have universal meaning. This is really no longer so today and this is why I want to give painting back its lost universality and anonymity, because the more anonymous painting is, the more real it is."[9] The painter's juxtaposition of the notions of anonymity and the real is unexpected and thought-provoking.

7

Jorge Luis Borges, *On Writing*, Norman Thomas di Giovanni, Daniel Halprin, and Frank MacShane, eds. (Hopewell, New Jersey: The Ecco Press, 1994), 53.

8

Balthus in Claude Roy, *Balthus* (Boston, Massachusetts, New York, and Toronto: Little Brown and Company, 1996), 18.

9

Op.cit.

Echoing Balthus, I propose that we also need to give architecture back its lost universality and anonymity, its essential timelessness, because the less subjective architecture is, the more real it is, and the more it has the capacity to support our individual identities. Our guide Rilke shares the view of the value of anonymity in art and creative work, in general, writing in a letter: "True art can issue only from a purely anonymous center."[10] Conversely, the more subjective a work is, the more it focuses on the limited subjectivity of the author, whereas works that are open to the world and to multiple interpretations will provide a ground of identification for others. There is a fundamental ethical difference between an architecture that exhibits its individual author and an architecture that aims at supporting the unknown inhabitant's individuality and sense of dignity. Just think of the assuring sense of the real evoked by the anonymous vernacular building traditions around the world. Why do we love to visit old villages and towns? Isn't it because we feel good in settings that support our sense of humanity and continuity in time?

Balthus also scorns self-expression as an objective of art, writing that, "Modernity, which began in the true sense with the Renaissance, determined the tragedy of art. The artist emerged as an individual and the traditional way of painting disappeared. From then on the artist sought to express his inner world, which is a limited universe: He tried to place his personality in power and used paintings as a means of self-expression."[11] It is interesting that the painter names the Renaissance as the beginning of modernity in art, whereas the movement is usually seen to originate in the mid-nineteenth century art or even the beginning of the twentieth. Again, the painter's concern clearly applies to architecture, although architects rarely write about the mental dimensions and aspirations in their work (As a sidenote, this is why I recommend writings by artists to my students, as artists usually write about their mental intentions and inspirations, not the technicalities or functional and formal aspects of their work.).

In Igor Stravinsky's Harvard lectures of 1939, published as *The Poetics of Music*,[12] the arch-modernist and arch-radical of music presents an unexpectedly forceful criticism of artistic radicalism and the rejection of tradition: "The ones who try to avoid subordination, support unanimously the opposite [counter-traditional] view. They reject constraint and they nourish a hope – always doomed to failure – of finding the secret of strength in freedom. They do not find anything but the arbitrariness of freaks and disorder, they lose all control, they

10
Rainer Maria Rilke, complete the note.

11
Balthus, op.cit.

12
Igor Stravinsky, *Musiikin poetiikka* (The Poetics of Music) (Helsinki: Otava Publishing Company, 1968).

13
Igor Stravinsky, op.cit., 75.

go astray [. . .]."[13] In the composer's view the rejection of tradition even threatens to eliminate the communicative ground of art: "The requirement for individuality and intellectual anarchy [. . .] constructs its own language, its vocabulary and artistic means. The use of proven means and established forms is generally forbidden and thus the artist ends up talking in a language with which his audience has no contact. His art becomes unique, indeed, in the sense that its world is totally closed, and it does not contain any possibility for communication."[14] Stravinsky's now-iconic 1913 composition *The Rites of Spring* was considered so radical for its time that its premiere in Paris turned into a violent cultural street riot; the event gives an added perspective to the composer's view of the dialectics of tradition and artistic radicalism.

14
Igor Stravinsky, op.cit., 72.

Again, newness and uniqueness alone are hardly relevant aspirations for art, as these criteria only deal with the surface characteristics of an artistic work. At the same time, to be emphatic on another front, I do not support historicist architecture either – those constructions that directly imitate a period style or set of appearances. For the record, I support a history-and-tradition conscious and critical architecture.

Meaningful artistic and architectural works are embodied existential expressions, and they articulate experiences and emotions of our shared human condition and destiny on an experiential and non-ideational level. Works of art – from poetry to music, theater to cinema, literature to dance, and painting to architecture – are metaphorical representations of the human existential encounter with the world, and their quality arises from the existential resonance and content of the work, i.e. its capacity to represent, and experientially actualize and energize this very encounter. To be more precise, artistic works do not symbolize another reality; they *are* another reality. As the great existentialist sculptor Alberto Giacometti wrote wisely: "The object of art is not to reproduce reality, but to create a reality of the same intensity."[15]

15
Alberto Giacomett, source unidentified.

16
Maurice Merleau-Ponty, "Cézanne's Doubt", *Sense and Non-Sense* (Evanston, Illinois: Northwestern University Press, 1964), 19.

Great works of art restructure, resensitize, and remythicize our encounters with the world. Merleau-Ponty suggests that Cézanne's paintings make us feel "how the world touches us."[16] A fresh and sensitized articulation of the fundamental existential and artistic issues gives an authentic work its emotive power and life force. An architecture that does not evoke sensations of life remains a mere formalist and esthetic exercise in composition. When art is seen in

its existential dimension, surface attributes and a self-consciously
sought uniqueness as formal qualities lose their value.

The essential relationship of a reverence for history and tradition,
on the one hand, and the achievement of artistic works of true
originality, depth, and significance, on the other, is advocated by a
veritable chorus across the disciplines and art forms. The Imagist
poet and editor Ezra Pound, generally acknowledged as a modernist arch-radical, also confesses his respect for tradition as he points
out the importance of the ontological origin of each art form: ". . .
[M]usic begins to atrophy when it departs too far from dance [. . .],
poetry begins to atrophy when it gets too far from music [. . .]."[17]
Octavio Paz, the great Spanish poet and essayist, also emphasizes the
meaning of song, music, and dance in the constitution of poetry.[18]

Similarly, in my view, architecture subsides into mere formal visually
based esthetics when it departs from its originating motives: domesticating space and time for human occupation, employing distinct
primal encounters – such as the four elements, gravity and materiality, and verticality and horizontality – as well as metaphorically
representing the act of construction itself. Architecture articulates
our conditions of existence, dwelling, and building. The process of
building is a kind of a dance – a ballet of construction labor. Without
a resonance with the timeless myths and traditions of building, architecture withers into a meaningless esthetic formal game.

Instead of attempting to portray newness, true architecture makes us
aware of the historicity of building and restructures our reading
of the continuum of time. In addition to the present, we need
to be able to live both in the past and in the future. Architecture
structures our understanding of the past just as much as it suggests
images of future – a perspective that is often forgotten or disregarded today. Every masterpiece reilluminates the history of the art
form and makes us look at earlier works in a new light. Old masterworks inspire later generations, whereas truly new works provide a
new frame of judgment for the experience and evaluation of the
works of the past through new modes of perception and understanding. "When one writes verse, one's most immediate audience is not
one's own contemporaries, let alone posterity, but one's predecessors," as the poet Joseph Brodsky asserts.[19]

This reverse causality of historical processes is the most interesting
and important, but usually history is read exclusively chronologically,

17

Ezra Pound, *The ABC of Reading* (New York: New Directions Publishing, 1987), 14.

18

Octavio Paz, "The verbal contract", *Convergences: Essays on Art and Literature* (San Diego, New York, London: Harcourt Brace Jovanovich, Publishers, 1987), 164.

19

Joseph Brodsky, *On Grief and Reason* (New York: Farrar, Straus and Giroux, 1997), 39.

20

Aldo van Eyck told about his lecture to the writer in a private conversation in the mid-1980s.

parallel with a common linear concept of the course of time. The modernist Dutch architect Aldo van Eyck approached historical process in this reverse fashion: asked by the Chancellor of the University of Delft to give his inaugural lecture as professor on the influence of Giotto on Paul Cézanne, Van Eyck politely refused and gave instead a lecture on Cézanne's influence on Giotto.[20] I find these reverse narratives, influences, and causalities frequently more interesting and inspiring than conventional linear chronologies.

Cultural identity – a sense of rootedness and belonging in a place and in a history – is an irreplaceable ground of our very humanity and mental well-being. Our identities are certainly in dialogue with our physical and architectural settings, but well beyond those settings as well, as we grow to become members of countless contexts and geographical, cultural, behavioral, social, linguistic, religious, as well as esthetic identities. Our identities are not attached to isolated things, but to the continuum of culture and life; our true identities are not found in momentary attractions but in their deeper, more durable historicities and continuities. Instead of being mere occasional background aspects, all these components of identity, and surely dozens of other features, are constituents of our personalities. The construction of our identity is not a given fact or a closed entity, but rather a process and an exchange.

21

Sarah Robinson and Juhani Pallasmaa, eds., *Mind in Architecture* (Cambridge, Massachusetts: The MIT Press, 2015).

22

Maurice Merleau-Ponty, "The Intertwining – The Chiasm", *The Visible and the Invisible*, Claude Lefort, ed. (Evanston, Illinois: Northwestern University Press, 1992).

23

Ludwig Wittgenstein, *Tractatus-Logico-Philosophicus eli Loogis-filosofinen Tutkielma* (Helsinki: Werner Söderström, 1972), 68.

24

Edward T. Hall, *The Silent Language* (Westport, Connecticut: Greenwood Press, 1959), and *The Hidden Language* (New York: Doubleday, 1966).

I settle in a place; the place settles in me. The recent neurological studies even show that our physical surroundings alter our brains.[21] Spaces and places are not mere stages for our lives, as space and mind are "chiasmatically" intertwined, to use a notion of Merleau-Ponty.[22] Ludwig Wittgenstein concludes concisely: "I am my world."[23]

The significance I am giving to tradition, not only as a general sense of cultural history and identity, but also as a comprehension of the specificity and locality of culture, raises critical concerns for today's practice of designing in cultures other than our own for commercial interests and gain. Anthropologists such as the American Edward T. Hall have convincingly shown that the codes of culture are so deeply ingrained in the human unconscious and pre-reflective behavior that the essences of culture take a lifetime to learn.[24] Do we really have the right to execute our designs in cultures that are very different from our own, merely for our personal ambition or economic interests? In this case, colonization of tradition, identity, and human mind – Isn't this just another form of colonization?

Let me be clear, I do not support nostalgic traditionalism or conservatism. I merely wish to argue that the continuum of culture is an essential – although mostly unconscious – ingredient in our lives, as well as of our individual identities and creative work. Creative work is always collaboration: It is not only collaboration with countless other thinkers, architects, and artists, but is also collaboration in the sense of humbly and proudly acknowledging one's role in the continuum of culture and tradition. Every innovation in thought – both in sciences and the arts – is bound to arise from the ground of and be projected back to this most honorable context. Anyone working in the mental and creative sphere, who believes that they have arrived at their achievement alone, is simply blindly self-centered or hopelessly naïve. In my lectures and writings, I always wish to set my thought in a cultural and historical context by my reference to an unusually extensive number of quotes.

Architectural and artistic works arise in the continuum of culture, and they seek their position and role in this continuum. Jean Genet, the French writer, touchingly expresses the idea of presenting one's work to the tradition: "In its desire to require real significance, each work of art must descend the steps of millennia with patience and extreme caution, and meet, if possible, the immemorial night of the dead, so that the dead recognize themselves in the work."[25] When a work of apparently extraordinary uniqueness is not accepted in this ever-expanding gallery of artistic traditions, it will be quickly forgotten as a mere momentary curiosity. Our time is usually building such momentary curiosities. On the other hand, regardless of its initial novelty and shock effect, even the most original and revolutionary work that succeeds to touch essential existential qualities ends up reinforcing the continuum of artistic tradition, joining it forever. This is the basic paradox of artistic creation: the most radical of works end up clarifying and strengthening tradition. As I already noted earlier, the Catalan philosopher Eugenio d'Ors gives a memorable formulation to this paradox: "Everything that remains outside of tradition, is plagiarism."[26] The philosopher's cryptic sentence implies that works of art that are not supported and continuously revitalized by the constant blood circulation of tradition are doomed to remain mere formal plagiarisms in the realm of arrogant and pretentious newness. These works do not have their roots in a cultural continuum; they do not possess an artistic life force, and, thus, devoid of roots, they are doomed to remain mere curiosities of the past.

25

Jean Genet, *L'atelier d' Alberto Giacometti* (L'Arbolft: Marc Barhezaf, 1963).

26

Eugenio D'Ors, as quoted in Igor Stravinsky, *Poetics of Music* and Luis Buñuel, *My Last Breath*.

The most eloquent and convincing literary defense of tradition is surely T.S. Eliot's 1919 essay "Tradition and Individual Talent," written 100 years ago; but its wisdom has been sadly forgotten. The poet states that tradition is not a static "thing" to be inherited, preserved, or possessed, as true tradition must be reinvented and recreated by each new generation. Instead of valuing mere factual history, Eliot argues for the significance of "a historical sense," an internalized mental dimension. This historical sense ties the artist and the architect to the continuum of culture and tradition, and provides the backbone to their artistic language and its comprehensibility. The fundamental issues of identity in terms of the questions "Who are we?" and "What is our relationship to the world?" are constitutive. This historical sense also brings about collective cultural meanings as well as a societal purposefulness. This historical sense gives profound works their combined humility, patience, and calm authority, whereas works that desperately aspire for novelty and uniqueness will always appear arrogant, strained, and impatient. Some of the greatest of masterpieces in art have patiently waited for centuries for their rediscovery on these merits.

Although Eliot's essay has been often employed as a reference, I wish to quote its most essential message, which is more pertinent today in the age of globalization than ever before:

> Tradition is a matter of much wider significance. It cannot be inherited, and if you want it you must obtain it by great labour. It involves, in the first place, the historical sense [. . .] and the historical sense involves a perception, not only of the pastness of the past, but of its presence; the historical sense compels a man to write [and to design] not merely with his own generation in his bones, but with a feeling that the whole of the literature [architecture] [. . .] has a simultaneous existence and composes a simultaneous order. This historical sense, which is a sense of the timeless as well as of the temporal and of the timeless and the temporal together, is what makes a writer [an architect] traditional and it is at the same time what makes a writer [an architect] most acutely conscious of his place in time, of his own contemporaneity.

> No poet, no artist of any art, has his complete meaning alone. His significance, his appreciation is the appreciation of his relation to the dead poets and artists. You cannot value him alone; you must set him, for contrast and comparison, among the dead.[27]

27
T. S. Eliot, "Tradition and Individual Talent", *Selected Essays*, new edition (New York: Harcourt, Brace & World, 1964).

In the last sentence, Eliot resounds the idea of the significance of the dead in artistic traditions, as earlier expressed by Jean Genet. The poet's arguments make it clear that true creative work is always bound to be a collaboration – a collective effort of the artist with their contemporaries as well as their predecessors. The views of the artistic thinkers provided here also demystify the myth of the solitary and isolated genius. This is a different dimension of solitude – a cultural one – than the individual mental solitude that Rilke writes about as a condition for creative work. Great works of art and architecture cannot arise from cultural ignorance; they emerge amid the evolving story of the evolution of the art form. The masterpieces emerge equipped with an inexplicable but endless capacity for dialogue and comparison.

Again, I do not praise tradition out of nostalgia; neither am I advocating traditionalism as an alternative to individual invention. I advocate for the embodiment of the essence of tradition and identity as a necessary precondition for meaningful creativity. I stress the value of tradition because of its fundamental significance for the course of culture and human identity, as well as for the arts, or any other creative endeavor for that matter. Tradition maintains and safeguards the collective and accumulated existential wisdom of successive generations, thereby providing a reliable direction and value to the new work, maintaining its comprehensibility and collective meaning. We can appreciate the genuinely new work of our own time because of Dante, Cervantes, and Shakespeare. At the same time, the masterworks of our time give new approaches and meanings to the masterpieces of the past, as Cezanne's art gave to Giotto in van Eyck's lecture.

Artistic meanings cannot be invented in a cultural vacuum, as they are unconscious and prereflective existential reencounters of primal human experiences, emotions, and myths. Our quasi-rational culture has abandoned myths and rituals, but these mental phenomena continue their existence in our subconsciousness. Alváro Siza, the Portuguese architect, argues, "Architects don't invent anything, they transform reality."[28] In the case of Siza himself, this attitude of humility has produced more lasting qualities in architecture than the self-assurance of most of his celebrated colleagues who have deliberately adopted the role of radical formal innovators.

The continuum of culture provides the ground from which arises all human meanings. Architectural meaning is always contextual, existential, relational, and temporal; it is never experientially an abstraction. Great works achieve their density and depth from the echo of the past, whereas the voice of superficial novelty remains feeble, incomprehensible, and meaningless.

28
Alváro Siza, as quoted in Kenneth Frampton, "Introduction", *Labour, Work and Architecture* (London: Phaidon Press, 2002), 18.

Tradition is mostly a preconscious system that organizes and maintains a sense of historicity, context, coherence, hierarchy, and meaning in the constant forward flow of culture. A coherence of tradition is created by the firm foundation of culture, not by any singular and isolated characteristic or idea. The quick collapse of this collective mental foundation during the past few decades is a serious obstacle for education today. It is difficult indeed, or often totally impossible, to teach architecture efficiently, when there is too little of the inherited tradition of knowledge in relation to which new knowledge could be understood. The dominance of digital search engines has led rapidly to the fragmentation of knowledge into detached, isolated facts and bits of information, reinforcing the lack of an integrating background of culture and giving rise to an equally rapid fragmented world view altogether. For philosophers of the Post-modern era, such as David Harvey and Fredrick Jameson, two of the disturbing characteristics of this moment are depthlessness and the lack of a holistic comprehension of the world.[29] A wide knowledge of classical literature and the arts has been a crucial ingredient of the understanding of culture as a background and context for novel thought and artistic ideas. How do you teach architecture and art when even the mentioning of almost any historically important name or phenomenon is met with a disinterested or even (innocently) unknowing gaze in response? Our personal identities are not objects, they are not things; our identities are processes and networks that build upon the core of an inherited cultural heritage. A coherent sense of self can only arise from the context of one's cultural heritage and its dynamic historicity.

In today's publicized and applauded avant-garde architecture, formal uniqueness is sought *ad absurdum*, at the cost of functional, structural, and technical logic, as well as of human perceptual, sensory, and mental realities. Architectural entities are conceived as ahistorical, detached, and disembodied built objects: detached from their context, societal motivations, and meanings, as well as their dialogue with the past. Eliot's essay is prescient in this regard, observing already in 1919 a "new provincialism," one just as visible in our time: "In our age [. . .] there is coming into existence a new kind of provincialism, not of space, but of time; one for which history is merely the chronicle of human devices which served their turn and have been scrapped, one for which the world is the property solely of the living, a property in which the dead hold no shares."[30] Here again we are reminded of the mental significance of "the dominion of the dead," in accordance with the title of Robert Pogue Harrison's previously cited book.[31]

29

David Harvey, *The Condition of Postmodernity* (Cambridge: Blackwell, 1990).

30

T. S. Eliot, "What is a Classic?", *Selected Essays*, new edition (New York: Harcourt, Brace & World, 1964).

31

Robert Pogue Harrison, *The Dominion of the Dead* (Chicago and London: Chicago University Press, 2003).

Societies and nations likely do not possess a capacity to learn; only individuals do, as learning is genetically coded in our individual heritage. Sadly, city after city, country after country, seems to go through the same fundamental mistakes that others, slightly ahead in cultural, technological, and economic development, have already committed earlier. In particular, the ecstasy of wealth seems to blind societies as well as individuals, compelling them to undervalue or neglect their own histories, traditions, and identities. In the case of newly wealthy contemporary societies, it is as if we would have become suddenly ashamed of our past, regardless of its human integrity and experiential quality of its settings, as if we would suddenly want to forget who we are and from where we have come. As the biologist Edward O. Wilson suggests, "our greatest problems arise from the fact that we do not know who we are and cannot agree on what we want to become."[32]

At stake in the loss of the lived sense of tradition is our very identity and sense of historicity. We are fundamentally historical beings, both biologically and culturally. We can reasonably think that we are all millions of years old; our bodies remember our evolutionary past by means of the biological relics in our bodies, such as the tailbone from our arboreal life, the *plica semilunaris*, the pink triangular point next to our eye where our horizontally moving eyelids were attached, when we were lizards in the Saurian age, and even the remains of gills in our lungs from our primordial fish life. Our mind is similarly historical and layered – an archeological site – as revealed by Sigmund Freud and Carl G. Jung, to which I have referred earlier.

In his book on slowness, the Czech writer Milan Kundera argues that forgetting is in direct relation to speed and remembering in direct relation to slowness.[33] The obsessively accelerated change of fashion and lifestyle in the contemporary moment makes an accumulation of tradition and memory mentally difficult, if not impossible. As Paul Virilio, the architect-philosopher, has suggested, the main product of contemporary societies is speed.[34]

The primary and eternal task of architecture is to defend and strengthen the wholeness and dignity of human life, and to provide us with our existential foothold in the world. The first responsibility of the architect is always for the inherited landscape or urban setting; a profound building always enhances its wider context, and gives it new meanings and esthetic qualities. Instead of degrading these existing contexts, responsible architecture improves the landscape of its location, and gives its lesser architectural neighbors new

32

Edward O. Wilson, *Biophilia* (Cambridge, Massachusetts and London, England: Harvard University Press, 1984), 37.

33

Milan Kundera, *Slowness* (New York: Harper Collins Publishers, 1966), 39.

34

Paul Virilio, *Katoamisen estetiikka* (The Aesthetics of Disappearance), (Tampere: Gaudeamus, 1994).

qualities and meanings. Profound buildings are not self-centered monologs, as they always engage in a dialogue with reality and the existent conditions. Buildings mediate deep narratives of culture, place, and time, and architecture is in essence always an epic art form. The content and meaning of art – even of the most condensed poem, minimal painting, or simplest house – is epic in the sense of being a manifestation of human existence in the world – an unbounded perspective of human consciousness.

The fascination with newness is characteristic to modernism at large, but this obsession has never been as unquestioned as it is in our age of mass consumption and surreal materialism. The designed aging of products, as well as the adoration of novelty, are deliberate psychological mechanisms at the service of accelerated consumption. In art's appeal to the momentary, it too now seems to serve the purposes of accelerated consumption and planned rejection. Architecture has also turned into a consumer product with a limited period of use, increasingly promoting and marketing distinct lifestyles, images, and personality types, instead of strengthening our sense of the real and of ourselves. These characteristics are ingredients of today's collective mental pathology.

The task of architecture is not to project dream worlds, but to create and reinforce essential causalities, processes of enrooting, and the sense of the real. The contemporary fascination with novelty is both cause and consequence of the self-destructive ideology of consumption and perpetual growth. Instead of contributing to meaningful and coordinated landscapes and cityscapes, the architectural structures of today's businesses stand as self-centered and self-indulgent commercial advertisements (And in the world of fluid global capital almost everything is considered business.). Whereas responsible buildings are rooted in the historicity of their place, and contribute to a sense of time and cultural continuum, today's monuments of selfishness and obsessive novelty flatten the sense of history and time. We are increasingly living in a flattened sense of nowness. This experience of flattened reality makes us outsiders in our own domicile. In the middle of abundance, we are becoming consumers of our own lives and mentally homeless. We are even becoming alienated from ourselves.

35
Herman Hertzberger, Addie van Roijen-Wortman, and Francis Strauven, eds., *Aldo van Eyck*, (Stichting Wonen/Van Loghum Slate, 1982), 65.

Yet, as Aldo van Eyck repeatedly insisted: "Architecture need do no more, nor should it ever do less, than assist man's homecoming."[35] Thus the need for an authentic architecture today. Great works of authenticity possess a timeless freshness, and they always present their enigmatic aura anew as if we were looking at the work for the first time: the greater the work, the stronger its resistance to time. Newness has a mediating role in revealing the existential dimension through fresh and unexpected metaphors. Only in the sense of the perpetually recharged and reenergized image, newness turns into timelessness, and becomes a quality in artistic and architectural works. This is where also anonymity turns into a specific value. Such works constitute the realm of tradition, and they are reinforced by the authority and aura of this very continuum.

I repeatedly revisit certain masterworks of painting, sculpture, and architecture, and re-read my favorite books, to find myself equally fascinated and moved each time. I have had the good fortune to visit the legendary Villa Mairea, designed in 1938–1939 by Alvar Aalto in Noormarkku, Finland, numerous times during more than half a century. At each new visit this architectural miracle welcomes me with the same freshness and stimulating sense of expectation and wonder. Aalto's masterwork weaves images of Finnish peasant life, Japanese traditions, modernist aspirations, and references to modern art into a synthesis that itself feels like the ultimate of traditions. In this work, as in all great works of art, tradition and newness are fused. The Villa exemplifies the power of a true artistic tradition that halts time and re-introduces that which is already known with a seductive new freshness and intimacy. The Villa embodies an architecture that empowers us, which strengthens our sense of being, dignity, and identity.

SENSORY THINKING   7
Peripheral Attention, Vagueness, and Uncertainty

Singular books or works of art can give a new direction to our entire thinking, work, and life, if we have the sensitivity to understand the new attitudes and the courage to act upon them. In my student years – the post-World War II period of the late 1950s and early 1960s – I was educated in the dominant modernist, rationalist, and positivist manner to see and think clearly and to seek precision and certainty. But in the mid-1970s, almost 15 years into my profession as an architect, I encountered two books (now practically forgotten) by the Austrian–British musician, painter, and scholar Anton Ehrenzweig,[1] one entitled *The Psychoanalysis of Artistic Vision and Hearing: An Introduction to a Theory of Unconscious Perception*[2] (1953) and the other *The Hidden Order of Art* (1970),[3] works, which had a profound and decisive impact on my thinking and awareness.

Ehrenzweig's psychoanalytical studies explained the insistent demand for precision in academic education and professional practices "as a defensive secondary process in a psycho-analytic sense."[4] He argued provocatively that creativity arises from vague, juxtaposed and diffusely interacting images, and unconscious perceptions and processes, not from focused perceptions or from precision and logical nonambiguity. Ehrenzweig's argument was an attack on everything that I had learned to believe. His convincing ideas transformed the virtues of my previous rationalist thinking into restrictions and handicaps. The challenges and conflicts of this encounter initiated my second intellectual and emotional life – a way of thinking and working that still animates me, and I will refer to his works extensively in this discussion.

I describe this pivotal moment in my life with great intention in the context of my discussions in this setting: to sound an alarm. I want to signal that our personal development will not necessarily be a smooth journey. That is also the message of our guide Rilke's words in his eighth letter to the young poet: "Why do you want to shut out

1

Anton Ehrenzweig was born and educated in Vienna, trained as a lawyer but he was deeply interested in modern art and music. He was also a recognized pianist and singer. After the "Anschluss" with Germany Ehrenzweig settled in England in 1938, abandoned his formal education and made a career as a lecturer in Art Education at Goldsmith College, University of London.

2

Anton Ehrenzweig, *The Psychoanalysis of Artistic Vision and Hearing: An Introduction to a Theory of Unconscious Perception* (1953) (London: Sheldon Press, 1975).

3

Anton Ehrenzweig, *The Hidden Order of Art* (1970) (Frogmore, St Albans: Paladin, 1973). Along with Rudolf Arnheim's *Art and Visual Perception,* and Herschel Chipp's *Theories of Modern Art*, Ehrenzweig's second book is considered one of the three classics of art psychology.

4

Ehrenzweig, op.cit., 1973, 59.

5

Rainer Maria Rilke, *Letters to a Young Poet* (New York and London: W. W. Norton & Company, 1993), 70.

6

As quoted in Ehrenzweig, 1975, op.cit. III.

7

Anton Ehrenzweig, "Conscious Planning and Unconscious Scanning", *Education in Vision*, Gyorgy Kepes, ed. (New York: George Braziller, Inc., 1965), 27–49.

8

Ehrenzweig, op.cit., 1975, VIII.

9

Ehrenzweig, op.cit., 1975, XI.

10

See Paul Klee, *The Thinking Eye* (London: Hutchinson, 1964).

of your life any agitation, any pain, any melancholy, since you do not really know what these states are working upon you?"[5] Together with Rilke, my advice is to be prepared for such pivotal moments, to be prepared to make abrupt and instant full turns in beliefs and intentions, as well as in the entire course of life.

As the motto of his first book, Ehrenzweig quotes the declaration of the pioneering American psychologist and philosopher William James: "It is, in short, the reinstatement of the vague to its proper place in mental life which I am so anxious to press on the attention."[6] This framing perspective shook the very foundations of my education and my newly acquired professional beliefs. Standing at the ruins of those beliefs, I begun to construct another mental world. Ehrenzweig's two books, as well as his essay entitled "From Conscious Planning to Unconscious Scanning,"[7] gave a new direction to my early interests in the mental foundations of artistic phenomena and the psychoanalytic approach to creativity – one that eventually also opened to me the phenomenological understanding of existential and artistic phenomena. I realized that an obsession with clarity, order, and rational, ideational meaning could be an obstacle to encountering and grasping the multiplicity and complexity not only of architecture, but moreover of life itself.

In the preface to that first book, Ehrenzweig makes the thought-provoking argument: "Art's substructure is shaped by deeply unconscious processes and may display a complex organization that is superior to the logical structure of conscious thought."[8] Although Sigmund Freud had published *The Interpretation of Dreams* already in 1900, I do not recall having heard the concept of "the unconscious" even once during my years of education in high school or university. Ehrenzweig suggests further that, "In order to become aware of inarticulate forms [artistic expressions that seep into the work past conscious intentionality and control] we have to adopt a mental attitude not dissimilar to that which the psycho-analyst must adopt when dealing with unconscious material, namely some kind of diffuse attention."[9] The layered and "polyphonic" structure of profound artworks – a structure that can be appreciated through "multi-dimensional attention" – has also been pointed out by artists such as Paul Klee.[10] Ehrenzweig emphasizes the significance of this layered quality and the merging of motifs, and points out that such an approach in artistic production and reception calls for a specific mode of attention. "All artistic structure is essentially 'polyphonic'," he writes, continuing "it evolves not in a single line of thought, but in several superimposed strands at once. Hence creativity requires a diffuse, scattered kind of attention that contradicts our normal logical habits of thinking."[11] The scholar also uses the notions of "all-over structure" and "or-or structure" to describe layered and vague artistic images.[12] This requirement for diffuse attention concerns the condition of both creative perception and thought.

A "diffuse attention" and an "empty" or "unfocused" gaze have gradually become my method of working, both in design work and in writing, and this approach has helped to emancipate my perception and thought from the constraints of dominating, constricting focus and rationality. When I work, I stare absentmindedly as if I had lost the focus and control of my mind. Only after having learned to confront my tasks as open-ended explorations without any preconceived ideas of the entity in question, or its essence and boundaries, have I felt capable of working in a manner that can lead to new grounds of perception, emotion, and thought.

A dynamic vagueness and an absence of focus are also the conditions of our normal system of visual perception, although we do not usually acknowledge it. Most of us who have normal eyesight tend to believe that we see the world around us in relative focus at all times. In fact, we see a blur, and only a tiny fraction of the visual field at any time – about one-thousandth of the entire field of vision – is seen distinctly. The field outside of this minute focused center of vision is increasingly vague and hazy toward the periphery of the visual field. Our focal vision covers about 4° of the approximate total angle of vision of roughly 180°. We are unaware of this fundamental lack of accuracy, because we constantly scan the field of vision with movements of our eyes – which for the most part remain unconscious and unnoticed – to bring a part of the blurred periphery at a time into the narrow beam of vision that is brought to a focal pinpoint at the fovea. Partly because we are deceived by this seeming physical ability for focused vision, our contemporary culture is a culture of focused, narrow, and fragmented attention, and we need to teach ourselves to become less focused and more aware of the dynamic multiplicity of visual signals we are receiving.

Experiments have revealed the surprising fact that our unconscious eye movements are not merely aids to clear vision but an absolute prerequisite of vision altogether. When the subject's gaze is experimentally forced to remain completely fixed on a stationary object, the image of the object disintegrates, and keeps disappearing and reappearing again in distorted shapes and fragments. "Static vision does not exist; there is no seeing without exploring," argues the

11
Ehrenzweig, op.cit., 1973, 14.

12
Ehrenzweig, op.cit., 1965, 28 and 30.

13

Arthur Koestler, *The Act of Creation* (London: Hutchinson & Co Ltd, 1964), 158.

14

Merleau-Ponty describes the notion of the flesh in his essay 'The Intertwining – The Chiasm' in *The Visible and the Invisible*, ed. Claude Lefort, Northwestern University Press (Evanston), fourth printing, 992: 'My body is made of the same flesh as the world . . . this flesh of my body is shared by the world [. . .]' (248); and, 'The flesh (of the world or my own) is [. . .] a texture that returns to itself and conforms to itself' (146). The notion derives from Merleau-Ponty's dialectical principle of the intertwining of the world and the self. He also speaks of the 'ontology of the flesh' as the ultimate conclusion of his initial phenomenology of perception. This ontology implies that meaning is both within and without, subjective and objective, spiritual and material. See Richard Kearney, "Maurice Merleau-Ponty", in Richard Kearney, *Modern Movements in European Philosophy* (Manchester and New York: Manchester University Press, 1994), 73–90.

15

Semir Zeki, *Inner Vision: An Exploration of Art and the Brain* (Oxford: Oxford University Press, 1999), 66.

16

Koestler, op.cit., 158.

17

Koestler, op.cit., 180.

Hungarian-born writer and scholar Arthur Koestler,[13] stating both a physiological fact and a philosophical stance.

I have already suggested earlier that our acquired image of the world is not a "picture," but a continuous plastic, polyphonic and multisensory construct that continuously integrates singular perceptions through memory and imagination. Our visual memory is not simply an archive of snapshots; on the contrary our visual perceptions are integrated and memorized as embodied haptic entities rather than singular retinal pictures. Finally, as I have already asserted in these reflections, the presence, permanence, and continuity of our experiential world is established and maintained as an embodied and tactile understanding of "the flesh of the world," a substantial encompassing comprehension that we share with our bodily existence.[14]

The recent neurological studies have revealed another surprising dynamic characteristic of vision. Experiments measuring the relative duration of time that it takes to perceive color, form, and motion show that these three attributes of visual perception are not perceived at the same time as a single neural entity at all. Color is perceived before form, which is itself perceived before motion, and the difference in time between the perception of color and the perception of motion is from 60 to 80 milliseconds.[15] This information by a respected neurobiologist was surprising to me, as I would expect our visual system to identify movement first, color second, and form as the last constituent of the image, on the basis of my assumption of their existential value in early human life. Aren't we warned first by movement, then by color, and last by form? Irregardless of my personal doubt, this scientific finding suggests that the different perceptual subsystems are functionally specialized and separated.

Arthur Koestler suggests a cautious analogy between visual scanning and mental scanning, "between the blurred, peripheral vision outside the focal beam, and the hazy, half-formed notions, which accompany thinking on the fringes of consciousness."[16] He argues, "If one attempts to hold fast to a mental image or concept – to hold it immobile and isolated, in the focus of awareness, it will disintegrate, like the static, visual image on the fovea [. . .] thinking is never a sharp, neat, linear process," and distinguishes focal awareness from peripheral awareness.[17] The disintegration of image is not limited to vision; even repeatedly pronouncing a familiar word, such as "mother", makes it gradually dissolve and lose its meaning; the meaning is in the instantaneous impact of the sound on our mechanisms of hearing and understanding, not an endless repetition.

This concept has its further implications for how we think and engage in creative activity. William James made a similar remark on the fundamental dynamism and historicity of thought: "Every definite image in the mind is steeped and dyed in the free water that flows around it. With it goes the sense of its relations, near and remote, the dying echo of whence it came to us, the dawning sense of whither it is to lead. The significance, the value of the image, is all in this halo or penumbra that surrounds and escorts it."[18] Thinking of this caliber took place in the very beginning of the last century; distressingly it has been forgotten in our obsession with rationality and focused thought.

Gestalt theory established the view of the articulating tendency, or *gestalt* tendency, of surface perception that selects and organizes images and their elements in accordance with distinct formal properties such as simplicity, similarity, compactness, coherence, and closure, for example. At the same time, the theory completely neglected the inarticulate form elements that are not part of the gestalt. Yet, more than a century ago, Sigmund Freud observed that form experiences arising from the lower levels of the mind, such as dream visions, tend to appear inarticulate and chaotic for the conscious mind, and they are thus difficult or impossible to grasp consciously. However, it is exactly this undefined, formless, and involuntarily interacting medley of images, associations, and recollections that seems to be the necessary mental ground for creative insight, as well as for the richness and plasticity of artistic expression.

Ehrenzweig establishes convincingly the priority of unconscious perception and thinking in the creative process. He even suggests that "any act of creativeness in the human mind involves the temporary paralysis of the [mental] surface functions and a longer or shorter reactivation of more archaic and less differentiated functions."[19] Instead of merely adding details to the multiplicity of artistic form, the inarticulate ingredients of the artistic language may well be its very origin and essence. Ehrenzweig argues further for the central importance of "gestalt-free vision" (modes of vision that take place outside the gestalt principles) and assumes that the capability of the superimposed perception of simultaneous and juxtaposed images implies that normal focused perception has to be suppressed. In accordance with Henry Bergson's views, he argues that "all creative thinking begins with a state of fluid vision comparable to intuition from which [. . .] later rational ideas emerge."[20] Ehrenzweig concludes that "all artistic perception possesses a gestalt-free element," and this "gestalt-free diffuse vision [. . .] is the artistic way of seeing the world."[21]

18
William James, *Principles of Psychology* (Cambridge, Massachusetts: Harvard University Press, 1890), 1983.

19
Ehrenzweig, op.cit., 1973, 46.

20
Ehrenzweig, op.cit., 1975, 18.

21
Ehrenzweig, op.cit., 1975, 35.

In his studies in the psychology of mathematical thought, the French mathematician Jacques Hadamard proposes that even in mathematics the ultimate decision must be often left to the unconsciousness as a clear visualization of the problem is usually impossible. Hadamard states categorically that it is mandatory to "cloud one's consciousness in order to make the right decision."[22] Hadamard makes an interesting further suggestion: "Greek geometry lost its creative impetus in Hellenistic times because of too precise visualization. It produced generations of clever computers and geometers, but no true geometricians. Development in geometric theory stopped altogether."[23] This suggestion that precision can become an obstacle for the creative flow of imagery casts a shadow on the exclusive use of precise digital technologies in the constitutive creative phases of design. We could exchange the mathematician's word "computers" in his statement into "computers," meaning our digital tools. Let me make a serious suggestion: The computer tends to define images too early with unwanted precision. I have also made the worried suggestion that the absolute metric precision of computerized design in architectural education and practice has a negative impact on the innately shapeless and measureless flow of images and ideas in human imagination.[24] In the creative phase of design, our ideas need to move freely, not to be caught in the nets of precise geometries and measures. A precise metric rendition for a vague initial idea is clearly a contradiction.

In his pioneering studies on the role of unconscious perception in creativity, Ehrenzweig shows how the two different manners of perception also apply to artistic hearing and music, where the surface gestalt of the visual arts is represented by the musical melody, which draws conscious attention to itself and also represents the memorized pattern of the musical piece. Yet music contains numerous inarticulate inflections of the melody – such as *vibrato, portamento,* and *rubato* – which are not articulate enough to be expressed by musical notation, although they contribute significantly to the emotional impact of music and are part of its essential structure. These inflections are left to the spontaneous execution of the performer.[25]

Outside the specific realm of artistic perception and creativity, an essential prerequisite for the everyday experience of the enveloping spatiality, interiority, and hapticity of the world is the deliberate suppression of sharp focused vision. We perceive and grasp overall entities and structures only at the expense of precision and detail. In fact, we have two separate brain hemispheres for this dual task.

22

Ehrenzweig, op.cit., 1975, 36.

23

As quoted in Ehrenzweig, op.cit., 1973, 58–59.

24

Juhani Pallasmaa, *The Thinking Hand: Existential and Embodied Wisdom in Architecture* (London: John Wiley & Sons, 2009), 95–100.

25

Ehrenzweig, op.cit., 1970, 43.

Yet, this important observation has hardly emerged in the theoretical discourse of architecture, as architectural theory and teaching continue to be interested in focused vision, strong gestalt, conscious intentionality, and the perspectival understanding of space. Additionally, most often architecture is dealt with as the construction of a material object or set of objects instead of as the evocation of sensory and mental experiences.

As is well known, the historical development of the techniques of spatial representation are closely tied with the history of architecture itself. Representational techniques reveal the concurrent understanding of the essence of space and vice versa; modes of spatial representation guide the understanding of spatial phenomena. The human system of sensory perception is a result of evolutionary processes, and determined and limited by our fundamental primordial existential conditions, whereas our intellect and imagination can engage in conceptualized spatial characteristics beyond the scope of direct sensory perception. Scientific constructs of multidimensional space that are impossible to visualize exemplify this extraordinary mental capacity. In addition to the complexity of the universe, cosmologists today speak of the multiverse – the possibility of multiple universes.

The lived human condition is always an "impure" or "dirty" mixture of a multitude of irreconcilable ingredients. As a multiplicity of perceptions and dreams, observations and desires, unconscious processes and conscious intentions, as well as aspects of the past, present, and future, the lived world is beyond formal description. As the consequence of this categorical "impurity" of experience, an authentic architecture is ultimately beyond objective, scientific description, and approachable only through live encounter and poetic evocation. This is the innate structural vagueness of human consciousness, and I propose a predisposing condition of creative work in architecture. However, as the design process itself in today's computerized practice is distanced from this "impurity," the very existential life force of architecture tends to be weakened or entirely lost, and design turns into cerebral and esthetic manipulation.

Since its invention in Renaissance time, the perspectival understanding of space has emphasized and strengthened the architecture of vision. By its very definition, perspectival space turns us into outsiders and observers, as it pushes us outside the realm of the object of focused perception, whereas simultaneous and haptic space encloses and enfolds us in its embrace, making us insiders and participants. In the visual understanding of space, we observe the space, whereas haptic space constitutes a shared and lived existential space. The quest to liberate the eye from its perspectival fixation has gradually brought about conceptions of multi-perspectival, simultaneous, haptic space, and multisensory atmospheres. This is the perceptual and psychological essence of Impressionist, Cubist, Color Field, and Abstract Expressionist painterly spaces, each of which employs methods that pull us into the very painting and make us experience it as insiders in an immersive embodied sensation. Visual space thus turns into an embodied and existential space that is essentially a dialogue and exchange between the space of the world and the internal space of the perceiver's mental world. This is the unique and personal existential space that we occupy in our lived experience. In an experience of place, particularly that of one's home, the external world and space become internalized; they are sensed as intrapersonal conditions, rather than as external material objects and perceptions. In all cases, our perceptions, our mental realm, and the world constitutes a continuum.

The heightened presence and emotive reality of profound artworks derive from the way they engage our perceptual and psychological mechanisms, and articulate the boundary between the viewer's experience of self and the world. Works of art have two simultaneous existences: their existence as a material object or as a performance (music, theater, dance), on the one hand, and as an imaginative world of image, memory, and ideals, on the other hand. The experiential reality of art is always an imaginative reality, and it is essentially a recreation by the viewer, the listener, the reader, or the inhabitant, as John Dewey taught us.[26]

26
See, John Dewey, *Art As Experience,* op.cit. (1934).

In architecture, likewise, the difference between an architecture that invites us to a multisensory and full embodied experience, on the one hand, and that of cold and distant visuality, on the other, is clear. True works of art and architecture immerse us in the complexities and mysteries of perception and the real world, instead of confining us in an alienating, constructed artificiality. In heightened emotional states, such as listening to music or caressing our loved ones, we tend to eliminate the objectifying and distancing sense of vision altogether through closing our eyes. The spatial, formal, and color integration in a painting is also often appreciated by dimming the sharpness of vision; the dynamic compositional totality can only be appreciated by means of suppressing detail.

The maximum color interaction in painting calls for a weak formal
gestalt that perceptually obscures the boundary of form, permitting
thus an unrestricted interaction of color fields across the perceptually weakly defined border. The interaction between figure and
ground in visual perception stands in inverse proportion to the
strength of the gestalt of the figure. The strong gestalt generates and
maintains a strict perceptual boundary, whereas liberated gestalt-
free perception weakens the structuring impact of boundaries, thus
permitting form and color interaction across boundary lines and
between ground and figure.

The vagueness and softness of boundary has yet another meaning in
creative thought, and that concerns the experience of self. In his essay
written in memory of Herbert Read in 1990, the author Salman Rushdie
points out the softening of the boundary between the world and the
self that takes place in the artistic experience: "Literature is made at
the boundary between self and the world, and during the creative act
this borderline softens, turns penetrable and allows the world to flow
into the artist and the artist flow into the world."[27] At the moment
of creative fusion, even the artist or architect's sense of self becomes
momentarily fused with the world and with the object of the creative
effort. In psychoanalytic literature this experience of sameness with
the world is frequently called an "oceanic" fusion or experience.

Creative activity and deep thinking surely call for an unfocused,
undifferentiated, and subconscious mode of vision, which is fused
with integrating tactile experiences and embodied identification.
Deep thought takes place in a transformed reality – a condition in
which the existential priorities and alarms are momentarily forgotten. The object of the creative act is not only identified and observed
by the eye, ear and touch, it is introjected (the psychoanalytic notion
for internalization of an object through the interior of the mouth
at the earliest phases of infancy) and identified with one's own
body and existential condition. In deep thought, focused vision is
blocked, and thoughts travel with an absent-minded gaze accompanied by a momentary loss of surface control of the existential
situation. For these reasons, deep thinking can usually take place
only in the protective embrace of architecture, in the "cradle of the
house,"[28] to use a notion of Gaston Bachelard, not in the unguarded
outdoors. Bachelard points out that architecture allows one to
dream in safety: "The chief benefit of the house [is that] the house
shelters daydreaming, the house protects the dreamer, the house
allows one to dream in peace."[29]

27
Salman Rushdie, "Eikö
mikään ole pyhää?" (Isn't
anything sacred?), *Parnasso
1*, (Helsinki, 1996), 8.

28
Gaston Bachelard, *The
Poetics of Space* (Boston,
Massachusetts: Beacon
Press, 1969), 7.

29
Gaston Bachelard, op.cit., 6.

Photographed architectural images are centralized and precise pictures of focused perceptions. Yet the quality of a lived architectural reality seems to depend fundamentally on the nature of peripheral vision and a dynamic interchange across the sensory field, and a deliberate suppression of sharpness that enfolds the subject in the space. Photographed imagery, particularly taken with wide angle and deep focus, are alien to the fundamental faculties of vision. Consequently, there is an evident discrepancy between architecture as experienced through photographs and a real lived experience, to the degree that imposing images of architecture in photographs often prove to be inaccurate and deceptive, rendering the architecture decisively less impressive when experienced live. In counterpoint, there are buildings that have such a powerful complexity, spatiality, and atmosphere – a fully realized and mediating quality – to the degree that photography cannot reveal their full essence.

A forest context, a Japanese garden, richly molded architectural spaces, as well as ornamented or decorated interiors, provide ample stimuli for peripheral vision, and these settings weave us as ingredients into the space and center us in it in a haptic manner. As we move our position in the space, even slightly, the unconsciously and peripherally perceived details and distortions invigorate the experience of interiority like an unconscious haptic massage. Regardless of the object-like externality and strictly bounded nature of our focused gaze and the continuous flow of individual fragmentary images, we sense the continuity and completeness of the space around us as an embrace. We even sense the space behind our backs; we live in worlds that surround us, not in frontal retinal images or mere perspectival pictures facing us. As I have suggested previously, our sense of reality is not primarily a pictorial experience, rather it is a "polyphonic" and simultaneous experience of all the senses at once; our experience of the world is more an integrated existential sense than a visual experience.

The preconscious perceptual realm, experienced outside the sphere of focused vision, is existentially as important as the focused image. In fact, there is medical evidence that peripheral vision has a higher priority in our perceptual and mental system. Ehrenzweig offers the medical case of *hemianopia* as a proof for the priority of peripheral vision in the psychic condition of our mechanism of sight. In a case of this rare illness, one-half of the visual field becomes blind while the other retains vision. In some cases, the field of vision reorganizes itself into a new, complete circular field of vision with a new focus of sharp vision in its center and a surrounding unfocused field. As the new focus is formed, the reorganization implies that parts of the former peripheral field of inaccurate vision acquire visual acuity, and, more significantly, the area of former focused vision gives up its capacity for sharp vision as it transforms into a part of the new unfocused peripheral field. "These case histories prove, if proof is needed," Ehrenzweig notes, "that an overwhelming psychological need exists that requires us to have the larger part of the visual field in a vague medley of images."[30]

These observations of the existential significance of unfocused peripheral vision suggest that one of the reasons why the architectural and urban settings of our time often project a weak sense of spatiality, interiority, and place, in comparison with the stronger emotional engagement of historical and natural settings, could be in their poverty of providing stimuli for peripheral perception. I suggest that in our modern world we live in a more focused world than was the case in earlier times. The fact that the human sensory world has dramatically changed through time has been convincingly argued in literature. This rather newly acquired precision could well have been supported by the central role of reading and pictures in our culture, both of which call for a focused and momentarily fixated eye. The visual experience of the world clearly has gained strength at the expense of auditory, haptic, and olfactory experiences, as demonstrated in Walter J. Ong's significant book *Orality and Literacy*.[31]

Unconscious peripheral perception transforms sharp and fragmentary retinal images into gestalt-free and vague spatial, embodied, and haptic experiences that constitute our full existential experience and sense of continuum. We live in a plastic and continuous world due to our dynamic system of perception, awareness, memory, and imagination that keeps constructing an entity of discontinuous fragments. Peripheral vision integrates us with space, while focused vision makes us mere ocular observers. In physical training, our physical skills are deliberately maximized for the purposes of the specific sport, but the mental processes of creative perception and thought are hardly touched upon in education. It is time to give vagueness its proper role in human consciousness as well as artistic and architectural education.

The issue of vagueness and indefiniteness is related with the notion of uncertainty. We are usually taught to seek certainty in our thinking and work, but a self-assurance and feeling of certainty tend to stop the flow of sensitive creative exploration, and, consequently,

30
Anton Ehrenzweig, op.cit., 1973, 284.

31
Walter J. Ong, *Orality and Literacy – The Technologizing of the World* (London and New York: Routledge, 1991).

32

Joseph Brodsky, "Less Than One", *Less Than One*, Joseph Brodsky, ed. (New York: Farrar, Straus & Giroux, 1998), 17.

33

Joseph Brodsky, "In Memory of Stephen Spender", *On Grief and Reason* (New York: Farrar, Straus & Giroux, 1997), 473, 475.

34

Joseph Brodsky, "On 'September 1, 1939' by W. H. Auden", *Less Than One* (New York: Farrar, Straus & Giroux, 1986), 340.

35

Joseph Brodsky, "*Less Than One*" (New York: Farrar, Straus and Giroux, 1998), 340.

turn counterproductive. Joseph Brodsky points out the value of insecurity and uncertainty for the creative endeavor: "In the business of writing what one accumulates is not expertise but uncertainties,"[32] the poet confesses, and likewise I believe that a true architect ends up accumulating uncertainties. Brodsky connects uncertainty with a sense of humility: "Poetry is a tremendous school of insecurity and uncertainty. . . [P]oetry – writing it as well as reading it – will teach you humility, and rather quickly at that. Especially if you are both writing and reading it."[33] This observation surely applies to architecture as well, and it is particularly humbling if you are both making it and writing about it. But the poet suggests that these mental states that are usually considered negative can be turned into a creative advantage: "If this [uncertainty or insecurity] does not destroy you, insecurity and uncertainty in the end become your intimate friends and you almost attribute to them an intelligence all their own,", Brodsky advises.[34] Uncertainty and insecurity are especially receptive states of the mind that sensitize it for creative perception and insight. As Brodsky clarifies, ". . . When uncertainty is evoked, then you sense beauty's proximity. Uncertainty is simply a more alert state than certitude, and thus it creates a better lyrical climate."[35]

I fully share the poet's views. In both writing and drawing, the text and image need to be emancipated from a preconceived sense of purpose, goal, and path. When one is young and narrow-minded, one wants the text and drawing to concretize and prove a preconceived idea, to give the idea an instant and precise formulation and shape. Through a growing capacity to tolerate uncertainty, vagueness, lack of definition and precise rendering, as well as momentary illogic and open-endedness, you can gradually learn the skill of cooperating with your own work, of allowing the work to make its suggestions, and take its own unexpected turns and moves. Instead of dictating a thought, the thinking process turns into an act of listening, collaboration, dialogue, and patient waiting. The work becomes a journey that may expose visions and ideas that you have never before conceived, or whose existence has been unknown prior to having been guided there by the work of your own hand and imagination, as well as your combined attitude of hesitation and curiosity fused together by genuine uncertainty.

There is an inherent opposition between the definite and the indefinite in art. An artistic phenomenon wants to escape definition until it has reached its self-sufficient existence. True creative fusion always achieves more than can be projected by any theory, and profound design always achieves more than the brief or anyone participating in the process could anticipate.

Since the foolishly self-assured days of my youth (a false confidence that disguised uncertainty, narrowness of understanding, and short-sightedness), I have come to realize that my sense of uncertainty has grown constantly to the degree that it has become nearly intolerable. Every issue, every question, each thought is so deeply embedded in the mysteries and uncertainties of both the world and of my own existence that often a satisfactory or resolved response or rendition does not seem to exist at all. Yet, life lived fully in the world resolves all contradictions: The principle of the world is balance, the finite balance of entropy, when all the forces are consumed. In a fundamental sense, I can say that instead of becoming a professional or an "expert," possessing immediate and assured responses, I have become increasingly more an amateur by age and experience, but an "amateur" understood in the loving and generous sense of that role and calling. A tolerance for uncertainty and vagueness can be learned, I have found; and these mental states that are normally seen as psychic and mental weaknesses and threats to one's sense of security and self can be converted to advantage in both work and life.

My pivotal encounter with the works of Anton Ehrenzweig was transformative. To this day, the approaches to the world resonate in my thinking, experience, and work, and I continue to find confirmations of these perspectives almost daily. I conclude this seventh reflection with a quote from Cornelius Castoriadis – the Greek–French philosopher: "What is most human is not rationalism but the uncontrolled and incontrollable continuous surge of creative radical imagination in and through the flux of representation, affects and desires."[36]

36
As quoted in Arnold H. Modell, *Imagination and the Meaningful Brain* (Cambridge, Massachusetts and London: The MIT Press, 2006, title page.

THE ART OF LEARNING   8
Learning, Unlearning, and Forgetting

During my architecture studies in Helsinki 60 years ago, my professor Aulis Blomstedt said in one of his lectures: "More important for an architect than the talent of fantasizing spaces, is the gift of imagining human situations."[1] This single sentence became the core around which my experiences and ideas of architecture began to revolve and coalesce – the essence of my lifelong education in architecture.

Architectural education has two complementary perspectives and goals: on the one hand, to develop an understanding of the discipline as a historical, cultural, artistic, technical, and professional practice, and, on the other hand, to develop the sense of self and identity of the aspiring architect. In my 50 years of experience in teaching architecture, educational philosophies, methodologies, and curricula tend to focus on the external phenomenon of architecture, and to undervalue the significance of the individual and inner mental reality of the student.

In my teaching, I have chosen to emphasize that mental ground of learning – of learning to become and to be an architect – more than teaching architecture as a given and objectified discipline. I have also become critical of the current increasingly professionalist attitude in architectural education as well as in architectural practice. The essence of architecture should be revealed through the student's process of maturation. In any studio or workshop in which I am engaged, I often tell my new students: "I am not going to teach you what architecture is, instead I will try to make each one of you aware of who you are," sometimes also adding, "Instead of teaching you architecture, I'll try to show you how to live your lives honorably as architects."

1

Lecture by Professor Aulis Blomstedt at the Helsinki University of Technology (currently Aalto University) in the early 1960s, memorized quote.

Rootedness: Reflections for Young Architects. First edition. Juhani Pallasmaa. Edited by Peter MacKeith.
© 2024 John Wiley & Sons Ltd. Published 2024 by John Wiley & Sons Ltd.

The enormously complex phenomenon of architecture must be confronted and experienced as an internalized personal encounter, rather than as an external object or a collection of facts. In addition to its utilitarian and practical purposes, architecture essentially concerns the enigma of human existence in this world. Thus, to grasp architecture, a student needs to become conscious of his or her own existence in the world. The first requirement for a teacher of architecture is to inflame the student's passion for architecture and to enable the student to see architecture in conjunction with life, especially the student's own life.

Architecture is not an end in itself; indeed, its purposes and meanings are beyond architecture. At the same time, the art of architecture relies upon the myths and traditions of architecture, and responsibly contemplates its own origins and evolution. Simply said: A building that does not reach beyond its utilitarian purpose is not architecture. On this basis, architecture is not a rational, logical, or clearly definable discipline; it is both "impure" and "messy," fusing and juxtaposing seemingly irreconcilable things, aspects, and attributes, such as scientific knowledge and personal beliefs, logical deduction and imagination, given factual parameters and mental aspirations, realities, and dreams. In 1955, the Finnish architect Alvar Aalto, newly appointed as a member of the Academy of Finland, pointed out this conflicting and contradictory ground of architecture in his inaugural speech: "Whatever our task[. . .] whether large or small [. . .] In every case, opposites must be reconciled [. . .] Almost every formal assignment involves dozens, often hundreds, sometimes thousands of conflicting elements that can be forced into functional harmony only by an act of will. This harmony cannot be achieved by any other means than art. The final value of individual technical and mechanical elements can only be assessed afterwards. A harmonious result cannot be achieved with mathematics, statistics, or probability calculus."[2]

2
Alvar Aalto, "Art and Technology", inaugural lecture as member of the Academy of Finland. *Sketches: Alvar Aalto*. Transl. Stuart Wrede (Cambridge, Massachusetts and London, England, 1985), 128.

Aalto's insight into architecture's need to fuse apparent opposites asserts persuasively that mere reasoning and rationality are insufficient for the architectural task. The internally conflicting phenomenon of architecture has to be approached and encountered through personal experience, imagination and intuition, self-identification, values, and an ethical sense. Only the act of experiencing, or "living," architecture can fuse the irreconcilable dimensions, aspects, and interactions into a coherent entity. Only through this internalized experience can the artistic or architectural phenomenon be encountered and emotionally grasped in its intended essence. This is the central message, again, of philosopher John Dewey's *Art as Experience*, as we recall from Chapter 1: "By common consent, the Parthenon is a great work of art. Yet it has aesthetic standing only as the work becomes an experience [. . .] Art is always the product in experience of an interaction of human beings with their environment. [. . .] The reshaping of subsequent experience by architectural works is more direct and more extensive than in the case of any other [. . .] They do not only influence the future, but they record and convey the past."[3] Significantly, the temporal continuum is emphasized here as an essential dimension of architecture.

Meaningful works of art and architecture are entire worlds – open and limitless images, probes, and mental excavations – which open up entire universes, universes "as reflected in a drop of water," as the Russian film director Andrey Tarkovsky describes the internal richness of poetic cinematic images.[4] The philosopher Jean-Paul Sartre likewise emphasizes the inherent openness of art: "If the painter presents us with a field or a vase of flowers, his paintings are windows which are open on the whole world."[5] An architectural work also is more than the material building; a true work of architecture confronts us with the world and our own existence. Such authentic work creates frames for perceiving and horizons of understanding the world, and compels us to sense our own existence with sensitivity and meaning.

The artistic image fuses the realms of beauty and truth, esthetics, and ethics. "Art is not a little selective sample of the world, it is a transformation of the world, an endless transformation towards the good," as our guide Rilke demands.[6] The most humbling description of the meaning of experiences of life and the significance of the embodied memory in artistic making is given by Rilke in his novel *The Notebooks of Malte Laurids Brigge*: "For verses are not, as people imagine, simply feelings [. . .] they are experiences. For the sake of a single verse, one must see many cities, men, and things, one must know the animals, one must feel how the birds fly and know the gesture with which the little flowers open in the morning."[7] The poet continues his list of experiences necessary for the creation of a line of verse almost endlessly: roads leading to unknown regions,

3

John Dewey, *Art as Experience* (New York: Putnam's, 1934), 4, 231.

4

Andrey Tarkovsky, *Sculpting in Time: Reflections on the Cinema* (London: The Bodley Head, 1986), 110.

5

Jean-Paul Sartre, *What is Literature?* (Gloucester, Massachusetts: Peter Smith, 1978), 272.

6

Rainer Maria Rilke. "Letter to Jacob Baron Vexhull, Paris", dated August 19, 1909. Rainer Maria Rilke, *Hiljainen taiteen sisin: kirjeitä vuosilta 1900–1926* (The Silent, innermost core of art: letters 1900–1926), edited by Liisa Enwald (Helsinki: TAI-teos, 1997), 41.

7

Rainer Maria Rilke, *The Notebooks of Malte Laurids Brigge* (London: W. W. Norton & Company, 1992), 26.

unexpected encounters and separations, childhood illnesses, and withdrawals into the solitude of rooms, nights of love, screams of women in labor, and tending the dying.

However, in the poet's view, even all of this together is insufficient for the creation of a line of verse. With this stunning and humbling advice, Rilke states that verses arise from remembered experiences, but that these experiences must be forgotten: "And still it is not yet enough to have memories. One must be able to forget them when they are many and one must have the great patience to wait until they come again. For it is not yet the memories themselves. Not till they have turned to blood within us, to glance and gesture, nameless and no longer to be distinguished from ourselves – not till then can it happen that in a most rare hour the first word of a verse arises in their midst and goes forth from them."[8]

8
Op.cit.

Education usually emphasizes memorizing, not remembering and forgetting; but the latter has deep significance in the creative process. Why should the emergence of an architectural idea be any easier or mentally less demanding than the emergence of a verse of poetry? If we consider architecture an art form of poetic power, why should the making of architecture differ fundamentally from writing verse, and why should it be less painful? Just as Rilke suggests for verse, deep architectural experiences are not mere esthetic fabrications or visual compositions; like poetry, they arise from a fundamental existential ground.

Architecture is constituted not simply by the internal requirements of the discipline; more fundamentally, architecture is rooted in our experiences of being in the world. In fact, architecture materializes, concretizes, and articulates aspects of our very humanity of our all-too-human vulnerability. I am sure every true architect, even you as beginning students, would confess to experiencing a feeling of being without a protective skin at the most subtle phases of design work. The inadequacies and shortcomings of the project at hand can often resonate with physical distortions or pains in the designer's own body.

In my view, in education a student crucially must confront experientially authentic things and entities from the very beginning, whether works of visual art, poetry, literature, architecture, or authentic and deeply felt human relations. A great teacher teaches primarily through their authentic persona, through the silent wisdom of their accumulation of lived life, and through their emotive presence, not primarily through the collection of facts that they have learned and accumulated. This is why great buildings and works of art can also be great teachers. The irreplaceable value of authentic experience is the reason why visiting real buildings and works of art is so important, and why this has been a significant aspect of learning for architects of the caliber of Le Corbusier and Louis Kahn (both of whose travels are so well documented), as well as for Glenn Murcutt, Tadao Ando, and Steven Holl.

Learning is a shared responsibility of the teacher and the student, and grades for schoolwork could just as well be given to the teacher as well as the student. In his essay, "What Calls for Thinking?" Martin Heidegger makes a remarkable comment on the difficulty of teaching: "Teaching is even more difficult than learning. And why is teaching more difficult than learning? Not because the teacher must have a larger store of information and have it always ready. Teaching is more difficult than learning because what teaching calls for is this: to let learn. The real teacher, in fact, lets nothing else be learned than – learning. His conduct, therefore, often produces the impression that we really learn nothing from him, if by 'learning' we now automatically understand merely the procurement of useful information. The teacher is ahead of his apprentices in this alone, that he has still more to learn than they – he has to learn to let them learn."[9]

9
Martin Heidegger, "What Calls for Thinking?", *Basic Writings* (New York: Harper & Row, 1977), 387.

When the American poet David Shapiro interviewed John Hejduk, the now-legendary Dean of the Cooper Union School of Architecture in New York (and surely one of the most dedicated and influential teachers of architecture in the past decades), and asked him about his teaching method, Hejduk answered: "I teach osmotically, by osmosis."[10] With this surprising answer Hejduk reveals the most essential manner of learning that learning is an unconscious, embodied, and existential absorption of ways of thinking and acting, rather than the intellectual and verbal recording of facts. This embodied immersion is also the way each one of us learned our mother tongue, for instance. I share my friend Big John's (as he was affectionately labeled) educational philosophy, and I have even used the same word "osmosis" to describe my own teaching approach, relying on an unconscious embodied absorption as the central learning process.

10
"John Hejduk or the Architect Who Drew Angels", Architecture and Urbanism, no. 244, January 1991, p. 59.

Hejduk articulated his educational method further: "I never draw for the student or draw over their work and I never tell them what to do. I try, in fact, to draw them out. In other words, draw out what's inside them and just hit a certain key point whereby they can develop their idea."[11] In true learning, serendipity and happy coincidence are as significant as any systematic study, subtle hints as important as information, and emotion as important as cognition. The systematic structure and content of the curriculum often differ fundamentally from the personal, subjective, and unique way an individual personality develops and the nature of the experiences that may prove significant for a student.

11
Op.cit.

In such a meaningful education we shape and mold ourselves, our very personality, character, and sense of self, instead of primarily accumulating facts, information and rules, or even skills. This modeling of self takes place predominantly through (to use Hedjuk's term) an unconscious embodied "osmosis," or to use the notion "mimesis," mimicking, of Plato and Aristotle. We usually associate mimetic learning with early childhood, but we all mimic unconsciously through our bodies and neural systems.

Our mimetic behavior has recently been illuminated by the discovery of the mirror neurons. These specialized neural units make us unknowingly mimic movements, gestures, and behaviors of others in our environment. New-born babies mimic facial gestures almost immediately; our openness to the world is given at birth. We also unconsciously mimic physical situations, events, objects, and qualities through embodied simulation. Art, music, and architecture can become parts of our very sense of self: a skilled musician plays himself rather than his instrument, and a masterful soccer player plays the entity of herself, the other players, and the internalized and embodied soccer field, instead of merely kicking the ball. "The player understands where the goal is in a way, which is lived rather than known. The mind does not inhabit the playing field, but the field is inhabited by a knowing body," writes Richard Lang commenting on the skill of playing soccer.[12]

12
Richard Lang, "The dwelling door: towards a phenomenology of transition", *Dwelling, Place & Environment*, David Seamon and Robert Mugerauer, eds. (New York: Columbia University Press, 1989), 207.

A life in architecture, and therefore any architectural task, must be similarly internalized, embodied, and lived, not just intellectually known or theorized. I can say sincerely, respectfully, that I learned more watching the way my professors walked and occupied space with their bodies than listening to their words. My professor Aulis Blomstedt's words notwithstanding, but I learned the very same lessons just by being in his presence. I want to make clear that I am not underestimating the quality of my education at all, although I can say that I learned more being with my mentors and breathing the same air than by doing what they told me to do in an architectural assignment.

We seem to be especially strongly influenced by the ethical air of our parents, friends, and teachers that we breathe in our youth. Our ethical judgment and conduct are not learned through books; rather these qualities are internalized in one's environment of growth, and they become a condition for self-respect. The essence of learning is the gradual construction of an inner sense of goals, responsibilities, empathetic imagination, ethical stance, and a combined sense of humility and pride, gratitude and generosity. In my view, while these polar attitudes are precisely the most difficult to acquire, our ethical sensibility is intrinsically linked with our esthetic sensibility. The poet Joseph Brodsky argues that the esthetic sensibility precedes the ethical one. "Man is an aesthetic creature before becoming an ethical being,"[13] he asserts, stating further that "Aesthetics is the mother of Ethics."[14]

The very essence of learning in any creative field is embedded more in the student's sense of self and their unconsciously internalized image of the world than in external and detached facts. The quality and effect of education is not measured by the quality of the syllabus itself, but by how effectively and deeply the education becomes absorbed by the student. Here, for the students' listening, don't misunderstand me! I do not question the importance of curricula and syllabi, and the philosophical depth in educational planning. I just wish to underline the fact that teaching is done by human individuals, and the intricacies of communication and interaction, mental impact and understanding, are also crucial.

This internal realm of learning can appropriately, but perhaps too dismissively, be called personal growth. Promoters of a fact-based professionalist education seem to dismiss this essential mental and existential perspective. Education – learning in any creative field – must address the student's individual and unique self. The meaningful, although mostly hidden, content of education needs to be more existential than factual, related more with experiences and values than information, more with ethical judgment than visual esthetics. Learned facts and skills only obtain their meaning in relation to the student's view of the world and themselves.

13
Joseph Brodsky, "An Immodest Proposal," *On Grief and Reason* (New York: Farrar, Straus and Giroux, 1997), 208.

14
Joseph Brodsky, op.cit.

Education methods tend to advance from basic elements toward complexities and larger entities. Yet there are no meaningful "basic elements" in artistic phenomena, only complete and lived images and experiences that provide the ground of meaning for the experience. There is much scientific evidence that we do not experience the world in these elemental dimensions so much as we experience holistic entities, experiences that project cohesive meaning onto the individual elemental understandings and present them as integrated wholes. As therapist and writer Iain McGilchrist states in his significant book on the interacting roles of the two human brain hemispheres, "[U]nderstanding is derived from the whole, since it is only in the light of the whole that one can truly understand the nature of the parts."[15]

In education, we are also usually advised to seek certainty and assurance; but accepting one's basic vulnerability and uncertainty may well be a more important mental orientation for a creative person. The feeling of certainty closes the processes of curiosity and investigation, whereas uncertainty keeps them constantly open. Certainty also tends to kill curiosity, and there is no creativity without curiosity. Again, Brodsky makes his position clear: "Poetry is a tremendous school of insecurity and uncertainty [. . .] Poetry – writing it as well as reading it – will teach you humility, and rather quickly at that. Especially if you are both writing and reading it."[16] In parallel, experiencing or making architecture will teach us humility. Great works of art and architecture simultaneously humble and dignify us.

Brodsky is also critical of the positive value usually placed on "expertise": "In reality (in art, and I would think science) experience and the accompanying expertise are the maker's worst enemies."[17] Surprisingly, he replaces expertise with uncertainty: "In the business of writing what one accumulates is not expertise but uncertainties."[18] Exactly the same happens in architecture. As a student and young architect, I knew exactly what a window or a door was; but now, after half a century of practice, I do not know any longer with any certainty. I need to rediscover the essence of the window and the door each time I design a house, as they had stopped being given "elements." The window is about seeing, observing, and being connected from the interior to the exterior. A window that focuses on a distant mountain top is a different window than the one that enables us to see an apple tree in the garden. A window is not its material frame, but the act of seeing and connecting through that

15

Iain McGilchrist, *The Master and His Emissary: The Divided Brain and the Making of the Western World* (New Haven, Connecticut: Yale University Press, 2009), 142.

16

Joseph Brodsky, *On Grief and Reason* (New York: Farrar, Straus & Giroux, 1997), 473–4.

17

Joseph Brodsky, "Less than One", *Less than One* (New York: Farrar, Straus & Giroux, 1998), 17.

18

Joseph Brodsky, op.cit.

particular aperture. Similarly, the door is not the door frame and door plate as technical "ready-mades," but the act of crossing the threshold between two realms: inside and outside; mentally, the most significant aspect of the door is the mental experience of the threshold – the crossing of a boundary. True architectural experiences are always verbs, invitations, and promises, not nouns; and, consequently, they are always contextual and unique. That is why, after my decades of design practice, I happily do not know anymore what a door or window is with any certainty.

Paradoxically, perhaps, the essence of learning is "un-learning", or forgetting the learned facts, as Rilke pointed out earlier. Instead of the word "unlearning," Gaston Bachelard uses the notion "non-knowing" for the mental condition of the poetic search for artistry.[19] Non-knowing was also the mental orientation of sculptor Eduardo Chillida when confessing that he had to face every new sculptural task through consciously forgetting his prior sculptures.[20] For Chillida, a new work was always totally different – a revealing confession of vulnerability from one of the finest, strongest artists of the last century.

I would also argue that architecture does not arise from theory, either. Architecture may, perhaps, arise from an experienced, then forgotten, and now embodied theoretical position. As I have written over 60 books, students repeatedly ask me what I gain in my design work from my literary or "theoretical" work. My sincere answer: "I only receive extra trouble." The trouble is the strengthened critical consciousness that tends to intercept the emotive and unconscious flow of ideas and images too early. I must also firmly confess that I do not really write "theory"; I am reporting on my perceptions, observations, experiences, and thoughts, instead of actually theorizing. My professor and mentor Aulis Blomstedt reminded me that the words "*theorein*" and "*theatai*" in the Greek language meant "to look at," not to speculate.

An intellectualized and overly conceptualized understanding of architecture pushes one away from the immersive identification with one's work, and tends to shift the work from an emotive and embodied involvement into a cerebral, intellectual, and external solving of a problem. Definitively, again I wish to say that architecture cannot be problem solving, as it is fundamentally an existential act and projection, not a definable "problem" to be solved. Architecture is more a personal confession, more an existential proposition than a

19

Gaston Bachelard, *The Poetics of Space* (Boston: Beacon Press, täydennä, 1969), 28–29.

20

Eduardo Chillida, Conversation between the sculptor and the writer, Helsinki 1989.

rational solution to a given problem. Again, I do not want to underestimate the intellectual and analytical approaches in architecture or in its education; but these approaches have their own niches in the overall constitution of the craft, and they should not be confused with the creative and emotive processes of design.

As I have emphasized throughout these reflections, we are complete biological and historical beings; and in any creative work we react with our entire existential sense and identity, rather than with our isolated intellect. In experiencing and making architecture, the most important sense is not vision in isolation, as educational practices normally assume, but our existential sense, through which we encounter, confront, and internalize places and settings as embodied existential experiences. We think with our bodies, muscles, and intestines as much as with our brain cells. Altogether, our relationship with the world is far more complex than we have understood. We are surely related with the world through more than the five Aristotelian senses; our physical, metabolic, neural, cognitive, and emotive systems have evolved gradually through millions of years of evolution, and it is evident that our deep physical and mental wellbeing is related with that immense evolutionary course of biology and physiology. Alvar Aalto's thinking in architecture was biologically oriented: "I would like to add my personal, emotional view, that architecture and its details are in some way all part of biology,"[21] and I can only agree with the perspective of my compatriot.

Earlier in these presentations I recalled the philosopher Ludwig Wittgenstein's suggestion that: "Work on philosophy – like work in architecture in many respects – is really work on oneself. On one's own conception. On how one sees things. And what one expects of them."[22] So too in architecture: we must construct and comprehend ourselves, and mentally construct and comprehend our world before we are capable of building places in which other people will inhabit, work, contemplate, or worship.

The poet T.S. Eliot asks in his 1934 poem, *Choruses from The Rock*:

> Where is the Life we lost in living?
> Where is the wisdom we lost in knowledge?
> Where is the knowledge we have lost in information?[23]

In educating creative capacities, information must be converted into knowledge, knowledge into existential understanding, and

21
Alvar Aalto, "The Trout and the Mountain Stream" (1949), *Sketches Alvar Aalto*, Göran Schildt, ed., Transl. by Stuart Wrede (Cambridge, Massachusetts and London, England, 1988), 97.

22
Ludwig Wittgenstein, *Culture and Value*, G. H. von Wright, ed. (Malden, Oxford and Melbourne, Berlin: Blackwell Publishing, 1998), 24.

23
Excerpt from T.S. Eliot, "Choruses from the Rock", *T.S. Eliot Collected Poems*, 1909–1962 (New York: Ecco Press, 1991).

THE ART OF LEARNING   107

understanding into internalized wisdom. And what is wisdom? Isn't wisdom the deepest quality of being human?

For me, the most eloquent and convincing advocacy of wisdom as the deepest quality of being human begins with Eliot's own defense of tradition in his 1929 essay "Tradition and Individual Talent," which I have already quoted and discussed at length in Chapter 6. But I refer to it again here in the context of "the art of learning" because its wisdom, so relevant to education, has been sadly forgotten today or else has collapsed under the pressure of consumerist society. In referring so emphatically to Eliot's assertions of tradition, I am neither praising tradition out of sheer nostalgia, nor am I speaking about traditionalism as an alternative to individual invention. Here I speak of the embodiment of the essence of tradition and cultural identity as necessary conditions for meaningful individuality and creativity. I defend the value of tradition because of its fundamental significance for the course of culture and human identity, as well as for the arts, or any other creative endeavor.

Tradition maintains and safeguards the collective and accumulated existential wisdom of successive generations. It also gives a reliable direction to the new, and maintains the comprehensibility and meaning of the new. Tradition is mostly a nonconscious system that organizes and maintains a sense of historicity, context, coherence, hierarchy, and meaning, in the constant forward flow of culture, whether it always implies progress, can well be disputed. A coherence of tradition is created by the firm foundation of culture, not by any singular and isolated characteristics or ideas. It is evident that artistic meanings cannot be invented, as they are mostly unconscious and prereflective existential reencounters of primal human experiences, values, emotions, and myths.

The dramatic collapse of this collective mental foundation during the past decades is already a serious obstacle for education in the creative fields today. It is difficult, indeed, or sometimes totally impossible, to teach architecture when there is no inherited tradition of knowledge in relation to which new ideas can be structured and understood. The rejection of books and the fragmentation of knowledge reinforces the lack of an integrating background of culture and gives rise to a rapid fragmentation of the world view. A wide knowledge of classical literature and arts has been a crucial ingredient of the understanding of culture as a background and context for novel thought and artistic creation. How do you teach architecture and art when the mentioning of almost any historically important name or phenomenon is met with an ignorant stare? Our personal identities are not objects; they are not things. Our identities are dynamic processes that are built upon the core of inherited cultural tradition. The productive sense of self can only arise from the context of lived culture and its inherent historicity.

As importantly, Eliot's arguments make it clear that creative work is always bound to be collaboration – a collective effort of the artist with their contemporaries as well as with their predecessors. The resonating views of the artistic thinkers that I quote in my lectures demystify the myth of the solitary and isolated genius. In my view, great works of art and architecture cannot arise from cultural ignorance; they emerge amid the evolving story of the human fate and the art form in question. Artistic and architectural masterpieces emerge equipped with an unexplainable capacity for eternal comparison and dialogue. The continuum of tradition provides the ground from which all human meaning arises. Architectural meaning is always contextual, relational, and temporal. Great works achieve their density and depth from the echo of the past, whereas the voice of the products of superficial novelty remain feeble, incomprehensible, and meaningless.

Possibly the most severe threat to humanistic and creative education today is the loss of the book, and, with it, the loss of a living tradition. Books – whether on poetry, novels, arts, philosophy, or the sciences – develop fundamental narratives of contextuality and causality, and open epic views into the continuum of culture and life. Regardless of the numerous advantages of digital media, their fluidity breaks narratives, causation, and logic into fragmented and unrelated bits of information, and the simulacra of the digital "space" strips away inherent human meaning, intimacy, tactility, and the sensuality of things.

The information in a book is not its primary value; the primary value is the book itself – the magical object and the epic logic of the narrative and its ethical causalities – that possesses the highest educational value. When reading, we keep imagining and constructing the cities, places, rooms, objects, and personalities – an entire fictitious world – based on the writer's suggestions. Great novels provide the most profound theater of learning about the logic and illogic, the ecstasies and frustrations, of life. Reading novels is not only a demonstration of our imaginative and empathetic skills, but it is also an exercise in these seminal skills. Literature permits us to view and experience life and its mysteries and dramas through the minds and hearts of some of the finest and most talented individuals of humankind. This is the great gift – the mercy of profound art and poetry – to us mortals.

Great architects, likewise, lend us the sensitivity of their skin to evoke "how the world touches us," to use the beautiful notion of Merleau-Ponty when describing the impact of Paul Cézanne's paintings. We can feel the touch of the world and culture through the skin of Luis Barragan or Louis Kahn, and experience the mysteries and veracities of existence.

Allow me to add one more observation about the magic of reading. As we read a poem, we internalize it; and we become the poem. When I have read a book and return it back to its place on the bookshelf, the book remains in me. Especially, if it is a great book, it has become part of my soul and body forever. In the same way, paintings, films, and buildings become parts of ourselves. Artistic works originate in the body of the maker, and they return to the body as they are being experienced. "In one sense, all art stems from the body," concludes Adrian Stokes, the British psychoanalytical essayist on art.[24]

24
Adrian Stokes, "Art and the Body" *The Image in Form: Selected Writings of Adrian Stokes,* Richard Wollheim, ed. (New York: Harper & Row, 1972), 122.

All art forms explore the existential essence of culture, life, and human consciousness, and all art is bound to follow similar aspirations, strategies, and metaphors. Art aspires to present the human condition and its essential existential enigma. Besides, all artistic expressions are sieved through the human senses, memory, and imagination. This view opens a bottomless well for architectural inspiration and insight to be sought through the study of other art forms. Because of its severe technical and logistical complexities and layered practical requirements, architecture tends to lose sight of its fundamental existential meaning, and turns into mere rationality or estheticization. An encounter with other arts certainly reinforces the architect's sensitivity to the poetic essence of their own art form.

Yet, the artistic tradition is not a depository from which to borrow, quote, or steal without permission. The tradition is an esteemed community of its own, a community of conversation, exchange, and mutual assessment and respect. Every art form has its traditions that have accumulated through millennia. You have heard me speak of the writer Milan Kundera, who insists on the "wisdom of the novel," and who argues that all good writers consult this wisdom. In his view,

25

Milan Kundera, *Romaanin taide* (The Art of the Novel) (Helsinki: Werner Söderström Ltd., 1986), 165.

26

Aldo van Eyck in a private conversation with the writer, 1982.

novels are always wiser than their writers, and writers who feel that they are smarter than their literary products ought to change their professions.[25] Often, when I listen to a self-centered and presumptuous colleague, I remember Kundera's advice and think: this architect should have changed professions.

Our works – provided they are authentic enough – also alter the reading of prior works. This reverse process of historical influence is often forgotten, but it calls for special sensitivity and responsibility. Aldo van Eyck, one of the seminal architects of the second-half of the twentieth century, who taught us the human meanings of geometry and showed the importance of anthropological studies for architecture, was asked to give his inaugural lecture as Professor of Architecture at the University of Delft on the influence of Giotto on Cézanne.[26] Instead of the suggested topic, van Eyck chose to lecture on the influence of Cézanne on Giotto; although the latter had died more than four centuries before the former was born. He realized that the thinking and painting of Paul Cézanne has made all of us see Giotto's work in a totally new context. I am mentioning this reverse interaction to emphasize the multidirectional and multidimensional nature of creative work. Creativity draws from and advances to all directions simultaneously, and new works keep constantly altering the old and revising our reading of history. True history is not written as a linear project progressing firmly toward the future, but rather backwards and forward, as a repeated cyclical process.

Architecture, as all artistic work, is essentially the product of collaboration, and architecture education in response would do well to emphasize this character and this lesson. The accomplishment of an authentic work of architecture, and the accomplishment of deep learning, is not only collaboration in the obvious and practical sense of the word, such as the interaction with numerous professionals, workmen and craftsmen, but it is a collaboration with other artists and architects – not only one's own contemporaries and the living, but also with predecessors who may have been dead for decades or centuries.

As a form of open-ended conclusion for this presentation on "the art of learning," I'll suggest that one's most important teacher of architecture may well have died half a millennium ago; and, in this sense, collaborative education in architecture is timeless, intimate, and demanding. I often instruct my students to be careful and ambitious in choosing their private mentors. You can choose to have Brunelleschi, Michelangelo, or Louis Kahn as your mentor, if you have the courage. The legendary Finnish designer Tapio Wirkkala told me that his real teacher was the Italian Renaissance painter Piero della Francesca, although the Florentine artist had died in 1492, 423 years before Wirkkala was born in the seacoast town of Hanko, Finland.

EPILOGUE
A Confession

As I described in the introduction, these reflections are based on
a series of lectures I gave in Fayetteville, Arkansas, at the Fay Jones
School of Architecture and Design in the spring of 2018. The lectures were initially conceived as being in dialogue with Rilke's *Letters
to a Young Poet* and addressed to an audience mainly of first-year
students in architecture and design. My talks to the students were
presented in a highly personal approach and emphasized a mode of
thinking that I identified for them as "phenomenological" – a way of
thinking about architecture that has been central to my own development and identity. To be clear, the lectures were not an academic
course in philosophy and certainly not in that specific branch of philosophy, but my emphases, references, and encouragements to the
students were situated in the context of a phenomenological understanding of the world and architecture's vital place in that world, as I
have come to understand that approach.

Most architects seem to experience phenomenology as a difficult
and vague philosophical approach, and of tangential value to work
in architecture. For both the students' sake, and for the sake of the
readers of these reflections now in published form, I decided to conclude with this "confession": a personal account on the development
of my design approach and work, and about architecture, arts, and
life, in general, with a particular thread throughout on the development of phenomenological thinking in my understanding of myself
and my undertakings in architecture. In this confession, I emphasize
the integration of work and life and one's personality and role as
architect. I wish to give you an example of how one can live one's life
as an architect.

My intention during my high school years in the 1950s was to
become a medical doctor – a surgeon, to be more precise. However,

Rootedness: Reflections for Young Architects. First edition. Juhani Pallasmaa. Edited by Peter MacKeith.
© 2024 John Wiley & Sons Ltd. Published 2024 by John Wiley & Sons Ltd.

when the time came to enter university, to my own surprise, I went to the entrance examinations of the school of architecture in Helsinki instead of the examinations of the medical school, as I had planned. I cannot recall at all what made me change my plans from studying medicine to studying architecture; it could have been the secret influence of our young, progressive art teacher during the two last years of high school whom everyone in the class admired. In retrospect, I have understood that the change in my career was not as dramatic as one would think; both the medical doctor and the architect attempt to improve the human condition – one in the intimate scale of the body, the other in the extended human, cultural, environmental, and collective body, and in both the cases, the hand – the feeling, understanding, and caressing hand – has a distinct role. For me, architecture is as much a phenomenon of the tactile and existential sense as it may be of vision, and that tactile and existential sense is what relates the work of a physician to the work of an architect.

I must say in all honesty that I never intended or deliberately decided to become an architectural writer or critic, not to speak of being characterized as a theorist or philosopher either. In the beginning of his *The Book of the Disquiet*, the great Portuguese poet Fernando Pessoa, who wrote under 52 pseudonyms (he would sometimes write a book under one of these pseudonyms and review it in the daily paper under another one), confesses: "I was a poet animated by philosophy, not a philosopher with poetic faculties."[1] As I have no formal philosophical training, I wish to paraphrase the poet's confession and confess: "I am an architect and author animated by philosophy, not a philosopher with architectural faculties." In the late 1960s, I drifted into writing without ever having made the deliberate decision to do so. I wrote my first short article in 1966, and during the past 20 years, especially since closing my architectural design practice, I have written an essay, a lecture, or an introduction to a book every second week – more than 25 texts every year. Altogether, I have now published over seventy books, and more than 800 essays and other writings. I cannot give any estimate of the number of lectures I have given around the world, surely several hundreds. All this to say that I continue to be animated by architecture, and it has a tempering and strengthening impact, resonating with and structuring my life experience.

As a beginning architect in the late 1950s, I was educated in the prevailing modernist, that is to say, rationalist, design

1

Fernando Pessoa, *The Book of the Disquiet* (published posthumously) (New York: Pantheon Books, 1991), 1.

methodology. I sought a scientific and logical grounding for my design work and thinking. In those early years, in parallel, I was especially interested in the visual arts and *Gestalt* psychology, and these interests also guided my views of architecture. During my two years of teaching architecture in the early 1970s at the Haile Selassie I University in Addis Ababa, Ethiopia, however, I lost my confidence in the modernist ethos – a worldview based on western rationality and on the unquestioned benevolence of technology, as well as on the universality of culture and thought. In Africa, I began to read anthropological, behavioral, and psychoanalytical literature. The studies by Edward T. Hall on the unconscious aspects of spatial behavior,[2] the research of Melville Herskovits and his team on cultural differences in the perception of visual illusions,[3] and the writings of Carl G. Jung,[4] Erich Neumann,[5] and Edward Edinger[6] on the subconscious mental functions and archetypes turned my thinking away from the predominant obsessive rationality of my education and culture. I became aware of the immense realm of the human unconscious and began to study the psychology of creativity.

After having returned to Finland from Africa in 1974, I became associated with a group of open-minded and progressive thinkers, which consisted of three Jungian therapists: the Dean of the Faculty of Philosophy at the Helsinki University, a philosopher/therapist and professor of the phenomenological orientation, a poet, a priest, a pianist, and two slightly older colleagues of mine. We convened a series of bimonthly conversations on life, environment, healing, and the arts, conversations which continued for 12 years.[7]

At the same time, I began to read the writings of the social psychologists Erich Fromm[8] and Herbert Marcuse,[9] as well as those of the therapist Alexander Lowen.[10] I was impressed by how these social psychologists could convincingly analyze the collective human mind and point out rather alarming distortions in our collective behavioral and cultural values and actions. Fromm's book *Escape from Freedom,* Marcuse's *One Dimensional Man,* and Lowen's books on the embodied mind were decisive for the development of my thinking about architecture. The mental diagnosis of the western industrial societies by Fromm and Marcuse, as well as Lowen's ideas on the hopeless narrowness of the linguistic communication channel in relation to the vast challenges and wisdom of the body, began to guide my thinking about art and architecture.

2

(a) Edward T. Hall, *The Hidden Dimension* (New York, London, Toronto, Sydney, and Auckland: Doubleday, 1966); (b) Edward T. Hall, *The Silent Language* (Garden City, New York: Doubleday, 1973); (c) Edward T. Hall, *Beyond Culture* (New York: Random House, 1976).

3

M. H. Segall, D. T. Campbell, and M. J. Herskovits, *The Influence of Culture on Visual Perception* (The Bobbs-Merrill Co, 1966).

4

Carl C. Jung (eds.), *Man and His Symbols* (New York: Doubleday, 1968).

5

Erich Neumann, *The Great Mother: An Analysis of the Archetype* (Princeton, New Jersey: Bollingen Series, 1972).

6

Edward Edinger, *Ego & Archetype: Individuation at the Religious Function of the Psyche* (Baltimore, Maryland: Penguin Books, 1974).

7

The conversations took place in the home of architect Keijo Petäjä and his wife in Helsinki in 1975–1988.

8

Erich Fromm, *Escape from Freedom* (New York: Henry Holt and Co, 1994).

9

Herbert Marcuse, *One-Dimensional Man* (Boston, Massachusetts: Beacon Press, 1951).

10

Alexander Lowen, *The Language of the Body* (New York: Macmillan, 1967).

Through this expansion of my thinking through reading, discussion, and reflection, I began to see the interactions and, eventually, the continuum of the mind and the world beyond the esthetic realm. I learned gradually to understand the interactions and fusions of the material and the mental worlds. I also began to realize that we are embodied beings, and that our body is foundational to the understanding of our relationship to the world. Thinking through the consequences of these realizations for my work in architecture, I began to realize that architecture is always in interaction with our entire being and with our existential sense, not only with our vision and cerebral faculties. Eventually, I comprehended that the body – our physical, substantial, sensing, responsive, emotional body – is a necessary component in thinking on architecture and working in architecture.

I describe my experiences and background to emphasize and concretize the value of having a wide enough perspective in one's interests and passions. Paradoxically, the width of your view will eventually also help you to focus – whenever precision and focus is needed.

11

Gaston Bachelard, *Poetics of Space* (Boston, Massachusetts: Beacon Press, 1969).

In the late 1970s, I encountered Gaston Bachelard's *The Poetics of Space*.[11] Daniel Libeskind, then the (young) director of the architecture studio at Cranbrook Academy, identified the book to me as one of the readings for his studio teaching. Bachelard's potent small book opened yet another new world for me – a world of poetic images and the interactions of the linguistic and material worlds. I became aware of the poetic and existential ground of architecture as opposed to mere visual esthetics. Inspired by Bachelard's approach, I began to read philosophers, psychologists of perception and creativity, and later, neuroscientists. As a side note, I wish to make the general comment that my path has frequently been directed by books and ideas suggested, pointed out, or gifted to me by my friends. Here, I remind the reader of the theme of my first lecture on the importance of friendships.

12

Juhani Pallasmaa, "Geometry of Feeling", *Encounters 1: Architectural Essays*, Peter MacKeith, ed. (Helsinki: Rakennustieto Publishers, 2005), 19.

In 1985, I wrote an essay entitled "The Geometry of Feeling"[12] – the title is, of course, consciously conflicting – which has later been republished as an example of architectural phenomenology in several international anthologies of architectural writings. I was made aware of phenomenology as a line of philosophical inquiry only while working on that very essay, and I hurriedly added a short section on this philosophical approach to my essay; this was the first time that I read about phenomenology and referred to it in my writing in an almost naïve and innocent introduction. Even today, due to my lack of formal philosophical education, I do not claim to be a phenomenologist. I rather wish to say that my current view of architecture and art is parallel to what I understand to be the phenomenological stance.

The expression "my phenomenology," my farm boy's phenomenology, seems most appropriate for this circumstance. The Dutch phenomenological psychiatrist J.H. van den Bergh argues somewhat surprisingly that "Painters and poets are born phenomenologists"[13]; similarly, I understand myself as a "born phenomenologist." My phenomenology arises from my experiences as a child, through my formative childhood observations and experiences in the early 1940s at my farmer grandfather's humble farmhouse, and then further as an architect, teacher, writer, and collaborator with numerous artists and scholars, as well as my travels and experiences of life, in general.

For me, phenomenology is a distinct way of looking at and understanding life and artistic phenomena. Edmund Husserl, one of the founders of phenomenological philosophy, used the notion of "pure looking" to describe the method of this mode of thinking in philosophy – an innocent and unbiased encounter with phenomena – in the same manner that a painter looks at a landscape, a poet seeks a poetic expression for a particular human experience, and an architect imagines an existentially meaningful place.

I have also realized that the meaning of the Greek words *theorein* and *theotai*s is to be looking at (the world or an object), not speculating (on ideas or concepts).[14] The phenomenologist looks at the phenomenon in question without *apriori* theories or prejudices and tries to identify himself with the phenomenon. My "theorizing" is an intense looking at things, or, rather, internalizing them in order to unravel their essences and meanings. In this, I am in sympathy with Johann Wolfgang von Goethe's view of science, which he called "Zarte Empirie (Delicate Empiricism)" – mode of thinking that aspires to observe without changing and violating the phenomenon in question.[15] As I write in the manner of literary associative essays, in which I have no hesitation to combine scientific findings with my experiential observations or perspectives of science with those of the arts, I do not aim at orthodox philosophizing.

13

J. H. Van den Berg, *The Phenomenological Approach in Psychiatry,* (Springfield, Illinois: Charles C. Thomas, 1955), 61.

14

I learned the meaning of the Greek word from my professor Aulis Blomstedt around 1965.

15

Johan Wolfgang von Goethe, *Scientific Studies* (Princeton: Princeton University Press, 1934), 307.

In my view, human cultures have three different categories for defining meaning for human existence: religion, science, and art. Religion and myths call for belief, science for rational knowledge, and art for emotive encounter and personal experience. In addition to having an interest in the interactions of these three categories, I wish to understand their fundamental differences. For the past four decades, this has been my way of looking at the world and its endless phenomena and, especially, of looking at architecture and experiencing its phenomenal effects.

As I have never studied philosophy academically, I am often uneasy about the fact that I am writing in a philosophical mode. I was both relieved and intimidated to be invited to join five internationally known phenomenological philosophers and writers, contributing essays to the book *The Intelligence of Place*, a set of studies on the philosophy of place edited by the Tasmanian philosopher Jeff Malpas.[16] After having submitted my essay for the book, I felt as if I had passed a philosophy exam.

16

Jeff Malpas, *The Intelligence of Place: Topographies and Poetics* (London: Bloomsbury Academic, 2015).

Thus, I must sincerely say that I am an amateur in philosophy, although I have read countless books by philosophers due to my personal interest in the enigma of human existence and consciousness and in the essence of knowledge. As I have mentioned earlier, my first philosophical inspiration was Gaston Bachelard, first through his book *The Poetics of Space*, and later through his other books on poetic imagery, especially on the four elements of air, water, fire, and earth. I was attracted to Bachelard's poetic writings early on because of their combined poetic evocation, precision, and sense of authority. The writer's long background as philosopher of science gives a special credibility to his poetic observations that sometimes seem to approach absurdity or paradox. Sincerity and precision are irreplaceable criteria and virtues in phenomenological thought.

Later, I have been particularly impressed by the writings of Maurice Merleau-Ponty, whose thinking I have found inspiringly open-ended, evocative, and optimistic. Merleau-Ponty's thinking has illuminated the way in which the inner mental and the outer material worlds intertwine "chiasmatically (the philosopher's phrase)," and that view has also opened to me multiple ways of understanding artistic phenomena. I have realized that many of the essential phenomena of life and art take place among established categories, disciplines, and empirical proofs, and can only be approached and understood through an innocent encounter with the phenomenon in question and with an open philosophical mind.

My phenomenological thinking began with an interest in the senses. This soon led me to a critique of the hegemony of vision in western culture, which had emerged already in Greek philosophy and has been dramatically accelerated by cultural conventions and technology. Consequently, architecture is usually presented as a visual art form. Through the phenomenological approach, I became aware of the significance of touch, particularly the unconscious hapticity concealed in vision. I also began to grasp the general "hatred of the body" in western thinking, to quote Max Scheler.[17]

As I described in an earlier lecture, we usually acknowledge the five Aristotelian senses; but Steinerian philosophy categorizes 12 senses, including the senses of self and being. After six decades of thinking, writing, and multifarious design work, I am convinced that the most important sense in architecture is not vision but our synthetic existential sense or the sense of self that naturally includes visual perception. As I have emphasized many times, we exist in "the flesh of the world,"[18] to use Merleau-Ponty's words, and architecture situates us in this very flesh. I have also become convinced that peripheral and unfocused perceptions are more important in architecture than focused perceptions. The continuous fusion of perceptions and things – the choreography of sensing – is more important than isolated singular images. Simply put, focused perceptions make us outsiders, whereas embracing, immersive, and diffuse perceptions make us insiders and participants. This proposition makes the formal dominance of vision and visually assessed esthetics in architectural theory and education questionable in comparison with a more comprehensive, existential, experiential, and atmospheric reading of architectural phenomena. I have touched upon these issues in my previous lectures and written a book length two-part essay – *The Eyes of the Skin* – with a more comprehensive argument and proposition.

We experience the world and ourselves in it in a simultaneous, synthetic, and multisensory manner. Merleau-Ponty expresses this simultaneity succinctly: "My perception is not a sum of visual, tactile, and audible givens: I perceive in a total way with my whole being: I grasp a unique structure of the thing, a unique way of being, which speaks

17

Max Scheler, *Vom Umsturz der Werte: Abhandlungen Und Aufsätze*, as quoted in David Michael Levine, *The Body's Recollection of Being*, Routledge & Kegan Paul (London, Boston, Melbourne and Harlem, 1985), 57.

18

Maurice Merleau-Ponty, "The Intertwining – The Chiasm", *The Visible and the Invisible*, Claude Lefort, ed. (Evanston, Illinois: Northwestern University Press, 1992).

19

Maurice Merleau-Ponty,
"The Film and the New
Psychology", *Sense and
Non-Sense* (Evanston,
Illinois: Northwestern
University Press, 1964), 48.

20

John Dewey, *Art as
Experience* (1934)
(New York: Berkeley
Publishing Group, 1980).

21

"Introjection" is a notion in
the psychoanalytic theory
and refers to the manner of
the newborn child to contact
the world through her mouth.

22

Maurice Merleau-Ponty as
quoted in Richard Kearney,
"Maurice Merleau-Ponty",
in *Modern Movements
in European Philosophy*
(Manchester and New York:
Manchester University
Press, 1994), 82.

23

Maurice Merleau-Ponty, as
quoted in Iain McGilchrist,
*The Master and His
Emissary: The Divided Brain
and the Making of the
Western World* (New Haven,
Connecticut: Yale University
Press, 2009), 189.

to all my senses at once."[19] Art and architecture are constituted in experience, which implies that ultimately the poetic dimension only exists in the lived individual experience. As I referenced in the first chapter, this was the crucial view of John Dewey.[20]

Perhaps surprisingly, I do not aim at, or believe in, a prescriptive verbalized architectural theory. Architecture is fundamentally existential in its very essence, and it arises from existential experiences and embodied wisdom rather than intellectualized and formalized theories. When we begin to work on a design task, we do not follow a theory, as we react to the task with our entire being: both mental and physical. We can only prepare ourselves for our work in architecture by developing our own persona, and a sensitivity and awareness for architectural phenomena; we need to identify ourselves with architecture. The act of looking at architecture implies, in fact, encountering and living architecture. A mere visual observation has to be accompanied by an imaginative and fully embodied experience by an identification and internalization of that experience. But multisensory experience is insufficient, rather a projection of oneself on the architectural setting and a simultaneous "introjection,"[21] to use a concept of psychoanalysis, must take place. The architectural spaces need to be internalized to become part of the viewer's sense of self. All profound artistic experiences are thus essentially exchanges among ourselves, our lived experience, and the world.

For me, phenomenology is the subtle art of encountering the world. "How could a painter or poet express anything other than his encounter with the world,"[22] Merleau-Ponty asks, and in my view, an architect is bound to explore, articulate, and express this very same encounter. Besides, the philosopher argues that the essence of art is always beyond it: "We come not to see the work of art, but the world according to the work."[23] I believe that I am an architect primarily for the reason that this craft offers particularly essential and meaningful possibilities of touching the boundaries of oneself and the world, and of experiencing how both the self and the world mingle and fuse into each other.

Salman Rushdie gives this fusion a particularly memorable foundation: "Literature is made at the boundary between self and the world, and during the creative act this borderline softens, turns penetrable and allows the world to flow into the artist and the artist into the world."[24] This surely applies to architecture.

Architecture is a logistically complex and philosophically controversial subject. The phenomenon of architecture contains several fundamental contradictions: utility and expression, technique and poetry, materiality and spirituality, durability and sensuality, esthetics and metaphysics, ethics and compassion – all at the same time. As architecture is simultaneously an end and a means, it cannot be prescribed, and it is bound to emerge through a creative process of compromise and synthesis. Due to its growing conceptual complexity in this ever more technological era, architecture is increasingly approached rationally as a task of knowledge, professional expertise, and problem solving. Consequently, the metaphysical, mental, poetic, and emotive realities of building are increasingly suppressed.

As a professional practice, architecture is increasingly understood as a service profession like engineering and law, and is increasingly losing its artistic autonomy and authority. The task of architectural philosophy is to reveal these biases and distortions in the prevailing view and practice of architecture. The phenomenological approach, which encounters architecture in its lived, real material and mental dimensions, is an important counterforce to today's formal, intellectualized, and estheticized, retinal and logocentric views that prevail in professional practice, theory, and education. Even though architectural phenomenology is bound to communicate ideas through words, the approach acknowledges and identifies the lived imageries hidden in architectural encounters and illuminates their experiential and mental impact and essence. A phenomenologist encounters and senses architecture instead of analyzing it, revealing the lived mental reality of this art form.

No approach or method on its own can be a guarantee for a meaningful result; phenomenology can degenerate into empty verbalism or groundless intellectual fabrication. As David Seamon, a phenomenological geographer who has written some of the most clear-minded descriptions on the use of the phenomenological method, wisely observes: "The phenomenological enterprise is a highly personal, interpretive venture. In trying to see the phenomenon it is very easy to see too much or too little."[25]

24

Salman Rushdie, "Eikö mikään ole pyhää?" (Isn't anything sacred?), *Parnasso*, (Helsinki, 1996), 8.

25

David Seamon, "A Way of Seeing People and Place, Phenomenology in Environment – Behaviour Research", *Theoretical Perspectives in Environment-Behaviour Research*, J. Wagner, J. Demick, T. Yamamoto, and H. Minami, eds. (New York: Plenum Publishers, 1999), 172.

I want to reemphasize that I write about architecture and the life-world as a practicing architect and designer – one who is also deeply engaged in the realm of the arts. I write in the same manner and with the same intentions that I sketch and draw – open-mindedly and without preconceptions or preset ideas. The words arise in the same manner as the lines of a drawing unfold, semi-automatically, revealing an image that has been hiding somewhere in the folds of thoughts, associations, and embodied memories. Both the line and the word, the drawing and the sentence, aspire to give a shape to an emergent feeling – a shapeless complex of uncertainty and intuitive assurance that acquires intentionality and meaning at the moment of its very emergence. Questions and answers arise simultaneously. Because of my way of working, a design task and an essay are very similar for me, even though they seem to be causally unrelated and exist in different realities as two parallel but independent products of observation and thought. Yet, both are connected in the existential experience.

Our spatial, material, and mental constructions provide the essential horizons of understanding our own being in the world. Everything merges into other things in a dreamlike manner in human consciousness. I read novels and poems, listen to music, look at paintings, and watch films as potential architectural propositions and sources of inspiration.

As an open-ended outlook to this last chapter, I confess that the aim of my writing is also my hope for the future. I hope that the next phase in responsible western thinking will question today's quasi-rationality, surreal materialism, and violent instrumentalization of knowledge. I believe that we are approaching an era of deep biological knowledge and ecologically contextual thinking. This new awareness will underscore the biohistorical and mental realities of human life, culture, and arts. It seems inarguable to me that our perceptual, embodied, and neural systems have developed the way they are to make us capable of processing existentially crucial knowledge and reactions in this very world that we inhabit. Consequently, even esthetics and ethics must be grounded in our biological historicity. Semir Zeki – the pioneer in the neurological understanding of art – confesses that he has set as his goal "to reveal the biological grounding of aesthetics."[26] With the assurance of a Nobel Laureate poet, Joseph Brodsky argues, "Believe it or not, the purpose of evolution is beauty."[27] This biohistorical and biocultural perspective – a

26

Semir Zeki, *Inner Vision: An Exploration of Art and the Brain* (Oxford University Press, 1999), 1–2.

27

Joseph Brodsky, "An Immodest Proposal", *On Grief and Reason* (New York: Farrar, Straus and Giroux, 1997), 207.

convergence both proposed by scientific research and asserted by poets, can also give a new significance to the central phenomenological position that seeks an essential mental interiority in our experience of the world surrounding our bodies.

In harmony with the origins of these reflections, here at the conclusion I confess to my hope for the restorative construction of the *Weltinnenraum* – the inner mental space of the world – to use the beautiful notion of Rainer Maria Rilke – our guardian angel in these journeys.[28]

28

Rainer Maria Rilke, *Hiljainen taiteen sisin – kirjeitä vuosilta 1900–1926* (The silent innermost core of art - letters 1900–1926). Transl. & ed. Liisa Enwald (Helsinki: TAI-teos, 1997).

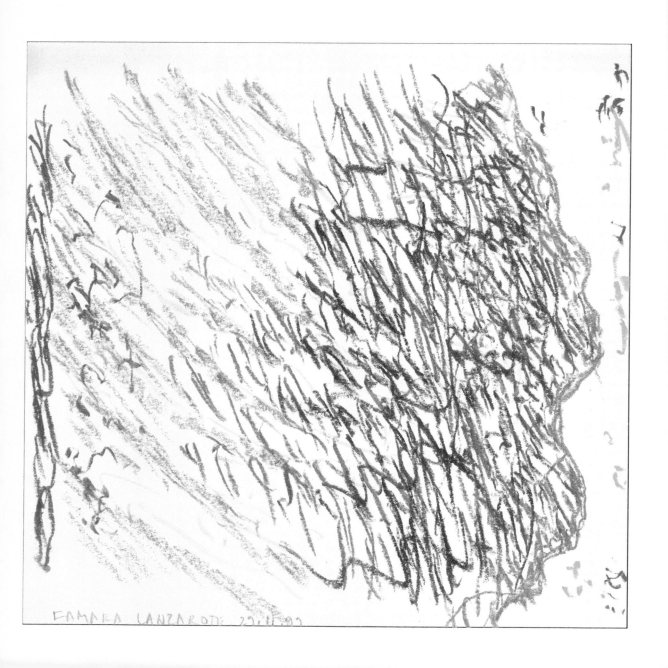

FAMARA LANZAROTE 29.11.93

RECOMMENDATIONS FOR FURTHER LEARNING
Books and Films

I have emphasized the crucial importance of experiencing authentic works of art, and reading great books and watching masterpieces of cinema makes this encounter available to anyone. The number of books and films today appears endless. A contemporary student might often feel helpless confronted with this infinite stream of words and images. What to read and where to even begin?

I have compiled lists of fifty books of literature and poetry, fifty books of philosophy and non-fiction, and fifty films of cinematic quality. My lists should not be seen as suggestions of the fifty best works of all time in the three categories. I have simply listed books and films that have been influential for my own thinking, and have established my views on the arts. I readily admit that my selections reflect the view of a Nordic citizen, born and raised in a particular era at a particular latitude, one who has been looking at the world culture and artistic events from that specific viewpoint. Many of these books I read during my student years and in the decades following; it is evident that I am a child of the mid-to-late twentieth century.

I also contemplated compiling similar lists of paintings and sculptural works, but as a visitor may experience hundreds of superb works on a single visit to one of the fine art museums in almost any capital or major city, I gave up this idea. Besides, as I have said, works of art should be encountered in their reality, not in reproduction, and a list of fifty recommendations would necessarily include works of art in many countries and museums. After having seen an art work "in the flesh," even a reproduction can bring back its true impact.

For a more comprehensive list of the most valued literature and poetry in the western world, I advise my readers to consult Harold Bloom's *The Western Canon: The Books and Schools of the Ages* (Papermac: London, 1996). I also recommend Professor Bloom's general guide to reading, *How to Read and Why* (London: Fourth Estate, 2001).

Rootedness: Reflections for Young Architects. First edition. Juhani Pallasmaa. Edited by Peter MacKeith.
© 2024 John Wiley & Sons Ltd. Published 2024 by John Wiley & Sons Ltd.

The year given after the title refers to the first publication of the volume. As many of the books have been published in different editions by several publishers, I have only given the title of each book without the publisher.

Fifty Novels and Collections of Poetry

Miguel de Cervantes, *Don Quixote* (published in two parts in 1605 and 1615)

Nikolai Gogol, *The Dead Souls* (1842)

Herman Melville, *Moby Dick* (1851)

Henry David Thoreau, *Walden* (1854)

Gustave Flaubert, *Madame Bovary* (1856)

Charles Baudelaire, *The Flowers of Evil* (1857)

Leo Tolstoy, *War and Peace* (1869)

Fjodor Dostoyevsky, *Crime and Punishment* (1866)

Fjodor Dostoyevsky, *Brothers Karamazov* (1880)

Anton Chekhov, *Steppe* (1888)

Rainer Maria Rilke, *New Poems* (1908)

Rainer Maria Rilke, *The Notebooks of Malte Laurids Brigge* (1910)

Thomas Mann, *Death in Venice* (1912)

Franz Kafka, *The Metamorphosis* (1915)

Franz Kafka, *The Trial* (1915, published posthumously 1925)

T.S. Eliot, *The Waste Land* (1922)

James Joyce, *Ulysses* (1922)

Rainer Maria Rilke, *Duino Elegies* (1923)

Thomas Mann, *Magic Mountain* (1924)

Marcel Proust, *In Search of Lost Time*, seven volumes (~1927)

Herman Hesse, *Steppenwolf* (1927)

Rainer Maria Rilke, *Letters to a Young Poet* (1929, published by Kappus)

William Faulkner, *The Wild Palms* (1939)

T.S. Eliot, *Four Quartets* (1942)

Pablo Neruda, *Canto General* (1950)

Vladimir Nabokov, *Lolita* (1955)

Wallace Stevens, *The Collected Poems of Wallace Stevens* (1954)

Junichiro Tanizaki, *The Key* (1956)

Alain Robbe-Grillet, *Two Novels (Jealousy and Labyrinth)* (1957)

Jorge Luis Borges, *Labyrinths* (1962)

Poems of [Anna] *Akhmatova*, Stanley Konitz and Max Hayward (1967)

George Perec, *A Void* (1969)

Ezra Pound, *Cantos* (1915–1962/1970)

Italo Calvino, *Invisible Cities* (1972)

Robert Frost, *The Poetry of Robert Frost* (1979)

Fernando Pessoa, *The Book of the Disquiet* (published posthumously 1982)

Paul Valéry, *Dialogues* (1989)

Milan Kundera, *Slowness* (1995)

Octavio Paz, *Selected Poems* (1957–1987/1991)

Jorge Luis Borges, *Selected Poems* (2000)

Paul Celan, *Selected Poems and Prose of Paul Celan* (2001)

Osip Mandelstam, *The Moscow & Voronezh Notebooks/Poems 1930–1937* (2003)

Federico Garcia Lorca, *Selected Verse* (2004)

Seamus Heaney, *100 Poems* (2018)

Antoine de St. Exupery, *The Little Prince*

Anton Chekov, *Short Stories*

Vincent van Gogh, *Letters to Theo*

Fifty Books of Philosophy and General Nonfiction

William James, *The Principles of Psychology* (1890)

Sigmund Freud, *The Interpretation of Dreams* (1900)

Wassily Kandinsky, *Point and Line to Plane* (1926)

T.S. Eliot, *Selected Essays 1917–1932* (1932)

John Dewey, *Art and Experience* (1934)

Erich Fromm, *Escape from Freedom* (1941)

Gaston Bachelard, *Water and Dreams* (1942)

D'arcy Thompson, *Growth and Form* (1945)

Jean-Paul Sartre, *What is Literature* (1948)

Jean-Paul Sartre, *The Psychology of Imagination* (1948)

Gaston Bachelard, *The Poetics of Space* (1958)

William Barrett, *Irrational Man: The Study in Existential Philosophy* (1958)

Edward T. Hall, *The Silent Language* (1959)

Gaston Bachelard, *The Flame of a Candle* (1961)

Paul Klee, *The Thinking Eye* (1961)

Joseph Albers, *The Interaction of Colour* (1963)

Maurice Merleau-Ponty, *Signs* (1964)

Carl G. Jung, *Man and His Symbols* (1964)

Herbert Marcuse, *One-Dimensional Man* (1964)

Henry Moore, *Henry Moore on Sculpture* (1966)

Edward T. Hall, *The Hidden Dimension* (1966)

Anton Ehrenzweig, *The Hidden Order of Art* (1967)

Walter Benjamin, *Illuminations* (1968)

Adrian Stokes, *Image on Form* (1972)

Henri Matisse, *Matisse on Art* (1973)

Edward S, Casey, *Imagining: A Phenomenological Study* (1976)

Martin Heidegger, *Basic Writings* (1977)
Junichiro Tanizaki, *In Praise of Shadows* (1977)
Susan Sontag, *On Photography* (1977)
Richard Sennett, *The Fall of the Public Man* (1977)
Ludwig Wittgenstein, *Culture and Value* (1980)
Edward O. Wilson, *Biophilia* (1984)
Elaine Scarry, *The Body in Pain* (1987)
Edward S. Casey, *Remembering; A Phenomenological Study* (1987)
Joseph Brodsky, *Less Than One* (1986)
Gianni Vattimo, *The End of Modernity* (1988)
Octavio Paz, *Convergencies; Essays on Art and Literature* (1991)
Joseph Brodsky, *Watermark* (1992)
Antonio R. Damasio, *Descartes' Error: Emotion, Reason and the Human Brain* (1994)
Joseph Brodsky, *On Grief and Reason* (1995)
Semir Zeki, *Inner Vision: An Exploration of Art and the Brain* (1999)
Mark Johson and George Lakoff, *Philosophy in the Flesh: The Embodied Mind and Its Challenge to Western Thought* (1999)
Jean-Paul Sartre, *Basic Writings* (2001)

Fifty Films

David Wark Griffith, *The Birth of a Nation* (1915)
Robert Wiene, *The Cabinet of Dr Caligary* (1920)
Sergei Eisenstein, *Battleship Potemkin* (1925)
Charlie Chaplin, *The Gold Rush* (1925)
Buster Keaton, *The General* (1926)
Luis Bunüel and Salvador Dali, *The Andalucian Dog* (1929)
Fritz Lang, *M for Murder* (1931)
Carl Dreyer, *Vampyre* (1932)
Jean Vigo, *L'Atalante* (1934)
Charlie Chaplin, *The Modern Times* (1936)
Jean Renoir, *Rules of the Game* (1939)
Orson Welles, *Citizen Kane* (1941)
Michael Curtis, *Casablanca* (1942)
Roberto Rossellini, *Rome, Open City* (1945)
Vittorio de Sica, *The Bicycle Chief* (1948)
Carol Reed, *The Third Man* (1949)
Jean Cocteau, *Orpheus* (1950)
Akira Kurosawa, *Rashomon* (1950)
Luis Bunüel, *Los Olividados* (1950)
Vittorio de Sica, *The Miracle of Milan* (1951)
Fred Zimmerman, *High Noon* (1952)

John Ford, *The Quiet Man* (1952)
Jasujiro Ozu, *Tokyo Monogatari* (1953)
Kenji Mizoguchi, *Ugetsu Monogatari* (1953)
Alfred Hitchcock, *Rear Window* (1954)
Ingmar Bergman, *Wild Strawberries* (1957)
Ingmar Bergman, *The Seventh Seal* (1957)
Jean-Luc Godard, *To the Last Breath* (1959)
Robert Bresson, *Pickpocket* (1959)
Alfred Hitchcock, *Psycho* (1960)
Francoise Truffaut, *Jules and Jim* (1962)
Andrei Tarkovsky, *Andrei Rublev* (1966)
Stanley Kubrick, *A Space Odyssey* (1968)
Andrey Tarkovski, *Mirror* (1971)
Bernardo Bertolucci, *The Last Tango in Paris* (1972)
Michelangelo Antonioni, *The Passenger* (1975)
Stanley Kubrick, *The Shining* (1980)
Andrei Tarkovski, *Nostalgia* (1983)
Peter Greenaway, *The Belly of an Architect* (1987)
Aki Kaurismäki, *The Man Without a Past* (2002)

Books by Filmmakers

As I have been impressed and influenced by the books of several film directors, I am listing a few of my favorites below:
Sergei Eisenstein, *Film Form: Essays in Film Theory* (1949)
Jean Renoir, *My Life and My Films* (1974)
Luis Bunüel, *My Last Breath* (1994)
Andrei Tarkovsky, *Sculpting in Time: Reflections on the Cinema* (1986)
Ingmar Bergman, *The Magic Lantern* (1988)
Federico Fellini, *Fellini on Fellini* (1976)

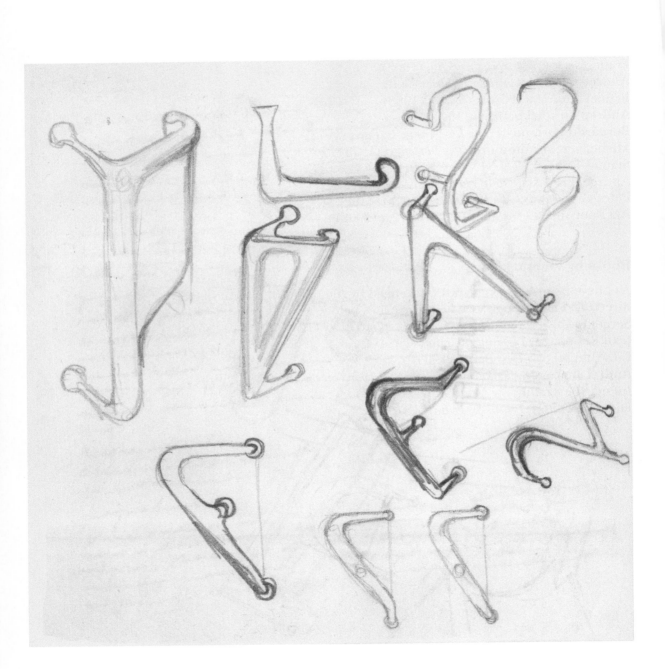

SKETCHES

The illustrations have been selected from thousands of sketches in the author's custom bound sketching books sized 225 by 225 mm. The size and square format were chosen because Pallasmaa frequently revolves the sketch book while sketching, especially when working on design ideas in bed. One and the same object frequently appears in different juxtaposed positions in a single sketch, as in sketch 5 of a seabird scull, and the sketches for door pulls.

As Professor of Architecture at the Aalto University in 1987–1993 Pallasmaa had similar sketch books made for the students in order to encourage them to sketch.

1. Tree protected from pests by a layer of lime wash by a road to Veracruz, Catemaco, Mexico. Color crayons, December 25, 1979.
2. Granite blocks connected by iron hooks against the power of ice, in the tiny village harbor of Hailuoto Island, Gulf of Finland. Black and color pencil, July 23, 1980.
3. Ruins at El Tajin, Veracruz, Mexico. The site includes over 150 buildings in various stages of erosion. Pencil and color crayon, December 1979.
4. Granite boulders by the sea on the Hailuoto Island, Gulf of Finland. Black and colored pencil, July 26, 1979.
5. Seabird scull, Stora Bergskär Island, Rosala islands, Southwestern Gulf of Finland. Pencil sketch, 1981.
6. Devil's Peak, Cape Town, South Africa. Color crayon, August 25, 1998.
7. Dogon Village, Bandiagara Canyon, Mali, Africa. Color crayon, 1978.
8. The village of Ait-Ben-Haddou, Atlas Mountains, Morocco. Color pastel, April 2012.
9. Pyramid of the Sun, Teotihuacan, Mexico. Color crayon, December 18, 1979.

Rootedness: Reflections for Young Architects. First edition. Juhani Pallasmaa. Edited by Peter MacKeith.
© 2024 John Wiley & Sons Ltd. Published 2024 by John Wiley & Sons Ltd.

10. White cotton grass, wetlands patch, Vänö Islands, southwestern archipelago, Gulf of Finland. The sketch was made on location at the painter Tor Arne's summer studio designed by Pallasmaa in 1979. Color crayons, August 1979.

11. Autumn colors in the Southwestern archipelago of the Gulf of Finland. Color crayon, 1985.

12. Eroding volcanic mountain, Famara, Lanzarote Island. Color crayon, November 29, 1999.

13. Sketches of door pulls. Pencil, early 1990s.